David Hill

David Hill studied at Victoria University, became a high school teacher, and worked in schools in New Zealand and the United Kingdom. He is an award-winning author of novels for both young people and adults. His writing for young people has been published and broadcast in the UK, New Zealand, Australia and the USA and translated into several languages.

Previous titles for young people include:
See Ya, Simon, Winner, Times Educational Supplement Nasen Award 1994 and the Gaelyn Gordon Award 2002; *Right Where It Hurts,* Winner, LIANZA Esther Glen Award 2003 and shortlisted for the New Zealand Post Children's Book Awards 2003; *Take it Easy,* Honours Award, Junior Fiction and AIM Children's Book Awards 1996.

In 2004, David was made a Member of the New Zealand Order of Merit and in 2005 he received the Margaret Mahy Award for Children's Literature.

This is a realistic and compassionate story... avoiding the cliché of the drunk teenager, opting instead to show what happens when a reasonably responsible but inexperienced driver loses his concentration long enough to cause a horrific accident that almost kills a girl.

New Zealand Herald

A powerful, heart-rending story of error and redemption, anger and forgiveness.

Taranaki Daily News

The stomach knots from page one of *Coming Back*, a convincing documentary-style story about everyone's teenage car accident nightmare.A gritty read about a boy facing tragedy with true courage.

The Dominion-Post

David Hill wastes no time introducing his two main characters with their alternating narratives, a structure that immediately builds interest, tension and suspense... a gripping, emotionally resonant story. Highly recommended.

Magpies Magazine

Every young adult who feels 10 feet tall and bullet proof when they get behind the wheel of a car should read *Coming Back*.

Marlborough Express

Despite its subject matter, this is a novel about hope, about budding romantic attachments, about developing one's talents, and above all, about supporting others. Recommended.

Tailspinner Magazine

This book is excellent for teens! I got so caught up in it that I just switched off to everything else. An absorbing story of friendship and family as well as hate and regret.

Grace Haack, Palmerston North Intermediate School

I would recommend *Coming Back* as a good book for 12 to 18 year-olds. Anyone can read the book and enjoy it.

Courtney Jones, age 14, The Mirror

DAVID HILL

COMING BACK

AURORA METRO PRESS

We gratefully acknowledge financial assistance from the Arts
Council of England and Creative New Zealand.

ARTS COUNCIL OF NEW ZEALAND TOI AOTEAROA

First printed in 2006 by Aurora Metro Publications Ltd.
www.aurorametro.com info@aurorametro.com
Coming Back © copyright David Hill 2004, first published in 2004
and published by arrangement with Mallinson Rendel Publishers,
Wellington, New Zealand.
Cover design: © copyright Joe Webb 2006 wwwetchdesign.co.uk
Production: Gillian Wakeling, Clare Chatham
With thanks to: New Zealand High Commission

Trade distribution:
UK – Central Books 020 8986 4854 orders@centralbooks.com
USA – TCG/Consortium N.Y. 212 609 5900 info@tcg.org
Canada – Canada Playwrights Press 416 703 0013
orders@playwrightscanada.com
Printed by Ashford Colour Press Ltd, UK

ISBN 0-9542330-2-6   9780954233020

*The author gratefully acknowledges the assistance
of Creative New Zealand and the Dunedin College
of Education.*

*Thanks also to Robin, Michael and Tineke Fancourt.
And to the brave Goldsworthys - Michelle, Colleen,
Graham, Brooke.*

CHAPTER ONE

RYAN:

If only. Two little words with one massive bloody meaning. If only.

I'd finished pretending to do my homework and was flicking through a *Tae Kwan Do* magazine when I heard Mum ask my stepfather Jon if he'd go down to the supermarket for her. I stopped flicking when I heard Jon say, 'Ryan can do it.'

Sweet, I thought. I'd had my restricted licence for just a fortnight, and every time I took the car out it felt so cool. I'd driven to the supermarket a few times when I only had my learner's licence, and I could feel Mum gripping the edge of her seat whenever I made the tricky turn out of the car park for the traffic lights. Now they trusted me to go by myself.

'Yeah, I'll do it,' I called, before my mother could say anything.

She was silent for a second, then, 'Can you go soon, please, Ryan?'

'There's plenty of time,' I told her. 'It's only half-eight.'

On a restricted licence, you're not allowed to drive between 10 pm and 6 am. Plus you can't carry any passengers unless they're a fully licensed driver keeping an eye on you.

Jon stuck his head through the doorway. 'Better go now, mate.' I muttered under my breath, but I knew he was right. Mum would be twitchy till I was safely back.

The phone rang while I was getting my jacket. 'Ryan?' Mum called. 'It's Vince.'

'I'll take it in my room,' I told her. Meet my sixteenth birthday present – my very own (I-nagged-for-it-for-months) phone extension. I closed my door and picked up the receiver. 'Whaddaya want?' I said.

My best mate laughed. 'A bit of bloody politeness for starters. Hey, you want to watch some DVDs tomorrow night?'

Tomorrow was . . . Friday. No *Tae Kwan Do* practice or anything. 'Yeah. Cool. What you got?'

'Ash and I are just heading down to look,' Vince said. 'Wanna come?'

'Can't. Gotta go to the supermarket for Mum. In the vee-hic-le.'

I should have known better. Vince was in like a flash. 'Pick us up, eh?'

Even though the door was closed, I lowered my voice. 'I can't. I'm on a restricted, remember?'

'Aw, come on,' Vince went. 'Nobody's gonna know. And it's chucking down outside.'

Crap. There'd been a few showers of rain since dinner time. 'I'm not supposed to take passengers,' I told him, and knew it sounded feeble.

Vince knew, too. 'What are ya? A bloody pussy? Ash and I can go to *Video Ezy* while you're Mummy's Boy at the supermarket. Come on!'

I could have said no. Instead I heard my mouth going, 'I'll pick you up at the bus stop.'

'Cool. Five minutes, eh?' The phone went down.

I got my jacket. I got the keys from Jon, and told Mum yeah, I'd be careful. I headed out to the garage and the *Subaru*. If only . . .

TARA:

It was such an awesome netball practice.

You know those times when everything works perfectly, when every pass goes straight to the right person, every shot curves through the hoop? This was one of those. Even Ms Gilchrist was pleased, though she didn't show it. Well, she wouldn't; she's a Maths Teacher.

We went through all our moves. The girls were really buzzing. Our team's called The Rockets, and we were sure flying like rockets. Brittany and Mel were burning all over the place. We were going to win the Summer League this term – no arguing!

There was one moment when Brittany threw a high pass and I jumped to take it. I felt myself soaring through the air, arms stretched out. I seemed to be hovering off the ground. I've been fumbling a few passes lately, but I caught this one perfectly, flicked it straight to Mel, and she sank another goal. Britt flashed me a ginormous grin. 'Awesome, Tara.'

'Not bad,' Ms Gilchrist admitted at the end. 'Team meeting tomorrow lunchtime, remember. And some of you also better remember your Maths assignment.'

Talk about coming down to Earth. Brittany and Mel and I all groaned together. Hell, I thought, I'll have to do it before I leave for work. 'I gotta go,' I told the others, and headed off for home.

I didn't bother to shower. No point, when you're spending the next few hours in a fish and chip shop. I did my Maths – sort of. I had a *Coke*, told Mum I didn't want any tea because Jimmy would give me some at work, didn't listen while she said that *Coke* and chips weren't good for an adolescent girl, Tara, and shot off with a wave to Dad, who was getting out of his car in the drive.

I zipped down to the corner, and over the pedestrian crossing on Lithgow Street. A car was coming, with only its parking lights on. It was closer than I thought, and the driver had to brake as I started out onto the crossing. He tooted at me as I made the footpath. I thought about giving him the finger, but I was still feeling so good from netball practice that I didn't bother. I started sprinting for Jimmy's.

RYAN:

Vince and Ash were in the shelter at the bus stop. Ash grinned. Vince said, 'Glad you remembered your mates,' as they piled in – Vince in the front, naturally.

'Just don't bloody tell anyone, eh?' I grunted. 'I want to keep this licence.'

I drove carefully, eyes open for cops. I told the others to crouch down if they saw any. So Vince squeezed down onto the floor, and started making police siren noises and waving his arms up above the dashboard. At the lights, an old guy in the next lane saw these two arms flopping backwards and forwards and locked his doors. When Ash told Vince, my best mate stuck a foot up in the air as well. Yeah, sometimes I wonder why he's my best mate.

We got to the supermarket. He and Ash poured themselves out of the *Subaru* and headed off for *Video Ezy*. 'Don't be long, eh!' I yelled after them. Hell, I sounded like my mother.

I got the stuff on Mum's list. I came back to the car, put the bags in the boot, and sat with the radio blaring on *Power FM*. No sign of the guys. My watch said 9.02 pm, and I was getting pissed off. It wasn't just that I had to be home by ten; Jon and Mum would be wanting to know what kept me so long. If I got stopped from using the car because of Vince mucking around . . .

I gave them another five minutes, then started the engine and drove out of the car park and across to *Video Ezy* – faster than I meant to. Vince and Ash were just coming out, and they didn't see me at first. When I blasted the horn at them, Vince made like he was in some movie, ducking behind a van outside the store, pretending to lob grenades at me.

'Come on!' I yelled. They jumped in. Ash said, 'Sorry, mate.' Vince said, 'Who's driving, then?' I gave him a filthy look, he stuck his hands up saying 'OK! OK', and we headed off. The rain was heavier now. 9.11 pm.

TARA:

It was a quiet night at the shop. Good for me; not so good for Jimmy.

Jimmy isn't his real name. He's Han Ze Minh, and he was a psychiatric nurse back in his own country. But when he and his wife Dolly came to New Zealand, our hospitals wouldn't give him a job till his English improved. So he's running this fish and chip shop for its owner, and learning English by correspondence. And from me, poor guy.

I saw a notice in their shop window about two months back: HELP WANT. THANKS YOU. I laughed, went in, got smiled at by this little pretty woman who said, 'Please now. Please now'. She called out in Chinese, and Jimmy came through from the back.

He's neat to work for. He and Dolly do the cooking. I take the orders, give change, chat to the customers. Jimmy listens and learns. Dolly listens and smiles. I work there Mondays and Thursdays.

Like I say, this Thursday was really quiet. Friday and Saturday are the busy nights. I don't work then, and I'm quite glad. You gotta have some social life, and anyway, too many guys come in half-pissed those nights.

At about five-to-nine, Jimmy said. 'You go, Tara. We can tidy.' Dolly nodded and smiled.

'You sure?' I said. Jimmy nodded, too. 'You go. Get pretty sleep.' I blinked, then realised he meant 'beauty sleep'. I'd have to tell Brittany and Mel that. 'See you Monday, then,' I told my boss(es), and they both grinned. I knew that when they closed, they'd go home to their grotty little concrete flat, and Jimmy would stay up for another couple of hours, learning his English.

Outside, it was dark and raining. I pulled up the hood of my parka and began to run. As I started, I snatched a look at my watch. 9.08 pm.

RYAN:

Vince was being a total dickhead. The DVDs he and Ash had got included some martial arts thing, and he was sitting in the passenger seat throwing *TKD* punches at the cars we passed. Jeez, I hoped nobody reported us to the cops. 'Cool it!' I told him. The rain was coming down quite hard.

'Drop us off at home, mate?' Vince said. 'We're gonna get soaked, otherwise.'

That would take another three minutes. Mum and Jon would be going ballistic.

Ash must have been thinking the same. 'It's OK,' he began. 'We can –'

Vince stopped him. 'Nah. Ryan's a mate. Aren't ya, Ryan?'

I grunted. I just wanted to get rid of them. I turned down Lithgow Street.

TARA:

The rain was driving down now. I didn't mind. I'd have a shower when I got home. Anyway, after the fish and chips, it was good to be outside where things smelt fresh and cool.

I kept my head down as I ran. My legs strode along. Brittany said she once heard a guy call me 'the chick with the great legs,' and I suppose they're not bad.

I came round a corner, skidded for a second on the wet footpath, then powered on. I was a Rocket. Nothing could stop me. I lifted my head, squinting into the rain, and saw the Lithgow Street crossing ahead. Only three minutes till home and a shower.

I looked down again as I ran. Aren't legs amazing? I suddenly thought. Not just mine, I mean. All human legs and the ways they move.

There was one car coming. It wasn't really close, and

anyway, I knew that tonight I could beat anything. I was a flying Rocket. I swung out onto the crossing.

The step down from the footpath was higher than it looked. I stumbled, and my foot slipped on the rain-slicked tar-seal. I staggered on the spot for a second.

At the same moment, the car's engine roared. From the corner of my eye, I saw it leap forward suddenly. Then it was on me.

RYAN:

Ash was getting pissed off, too. 'Give it a rest, Vince!' But Vince took no notice. 'I am a fighting machine. The ultimate ninja. Hee-ya!' His hand punched the air in front of me.

I ignored him. Just let me drop these two off, and try to think up an excuse for Mum and Jon.

We came round a corner. Vince held the DVD now, and was pretending to throw it like a Kung-Fu star. Suddenly I'd had enough. I shoved him sideways, grabbed the DVD out of his hand, and yelled, 'Just bloody cool it!' I half-turned, to drop the DVD on the back seat beside Ash.

As I did so, my right foot slipped on the accelerator. The engine revved, and the car shot forward. For half a second, my eyes met Ash's. He was staring past me, through the front windscreen. He began to yell something.

Somehow I knew what it was. I wrenched my head round, foot stabbing for the brake. And there was the girl, right in front of us.

CHAPTER TWO

A violent blow to the head may cause a sudden movement of the brain inside the skull. This may result in tearing of brain tissue, plus microscopic bleeding and possible structural damage. Nerve cell connections will probably be severed, and impulses cannot be transmitted. The result is various levels of unconsciousness, or (if damage is severe) extensive loss of brain functions including complete brain death.

RYAN:

In the headlights, I saw her face. Brown hair, swinging as she turned to stare at us. Brown eyes, stretched wide and startled. Then she hit the windscreen.

The *Subaru* seemed to scoop her up and throw her at us. Her head hit the glass between me and Vince. There was this Thok! sound, like a basketball smacking down on the floor. Then the windscreen broke. Oh, Christ, HER HEAD BROKE THE WINDSCREEN.

Lines ran across the glass in all directions. The screen began crumbling, dissolving, dropping in little bits onto the dashboard. I couldn't see a thing.

Beside me, Vince was yelling, 'Oh shit! Oh shit!' Ash's hands gripped the back of my seat so hard, I thought he was going to tear it off.

My arms and legs had gone as stiff as steel rods. My right foot was jammed on the brake, and I heard the tyres shriek and slip on the wet road. Vince and I were flung forwards against the seatbelts. Blind behind the crazed, cracked windscreen, I twisted the steering wheel. The car slewed sideways, smacked into the kerb and stopped. The engine stalled.

For two seconds maybe, we sat there in complete silence. I already knew that I'd done the very worst thing in the world.

TARA:

The front of the car hit me and knocked the wind out of me. I felt myself lifted up. For a moment, I saw these two guys' faces gaping at me. They looked totally stupid – like guys often do – and scared shitless.

Another weird thought skidded through my mind. I haven't had a shower. If I'm hurt and I have to see a doctor, I'm going to pong.

My head filled with heat suddenly. Red, swelling heat, trying to burst out. I heard a roaring, shuddering noise. I was in mid-air, arms and legs stretched out.

Then everything – the car, the guys, me – went rushing and shrinking together in a tiny glare of light, and I sank into the dark.

RYAN:

The silence in the car didn't last. Vince started mouthing again. 'Oh no! Oh shit!' I felt wild at him for being such a dork.

I started heaving at the door to get out. The windscreen was like a cracked ice sheet in front of me. I couldn't tell if the girl was on the bonnet, or on the road, or what.

I was halfway out when Ash grabbed me. 'The hazard lights! Put the hazard lights on!' I reached out and pressed the switch. The car door swung back shut, and little lumps of windscreen collapsed into my lap. Jon is going to be so pissed off, a corner of my mind told me stupidly.

I stepped out into the rain and darkness. The lights of the pedestrian crossing blinked on-off, on-off. Nothing on the bonnet. Nothing on the ground in front of the car. I even checked the roof and the road behind, feeling my hands squeeze into fists as I looked. No sign. The girl had vanished.

A wild hope rushed up in me. She'd taken off. She'd been so embarrassed that she didn't want to talk to anyone, and she'd taken off.

Even as I thought it, I knew it wasn't true. And right then, Ash grabbed my arm and pointed ahead. 'There!'

It couldn't be. It couldn't. The dark huddle on the road was twenty metres away, as far as a bloody cricket pitch. She couldn't have been thrown that far.

'Come on!' Ash sprinted towards her. Vince ran too, babbling, 'I'm sorry, mate! Jeez, I'm sorry!' I stood locked still for a half-second, then set off after them. But I knew it was useless. I knew she was dead.

TARA:
Far away, I felt something rough against my cheek. Rough and wet: I must have fallen over in the shower. My side hurt. Terror rose inside me, like some creature

trying to escape. Then the shrinking and the nothing-ness again.

RYAN:

The darkness and the way she was lying meant I couldn't see her properly. There was blood in the brown hair, but not much. Maybe –? The sleeve of her parka was ripped, and her T-shirt was pulled up, showing a curve of bare, smooth back with the rain falling on it.

I wanted to keep her dry, as if that would somehow make everything OK. I dragged off my jacket, and knelt to spread it over her. 'Don't touch her!' Ash went. 'Don't move her!'

I'm not bloody leaving her – I thought. A car sped past, horn blaring at us where we crouched in the road. 'Stupid bastards!' yelled Vince. 'You'll hit –' He twisted to look at the girl again. 'Oh, Christ!'

I started to snarl something at him. If he hadn't been mucking around – coldness swelled inside me. I laid my jacket over the tumbled shape. More headlights were coming towards us. My body felt stiff and heavy, but I forced myself forward, arms waving. The car slowed and stopped. A guy peered at me suspiciously through the side window.

'A cellphone?' I shouted. 'You got a cellphone? There's a girl hurt.'

The guy took another look at me, then his window slid down. 'You need an ambulance?'

'Yeah. Quick. As quick as they can.' But it wasn't going to do any good. It was too late.

Another car went past, dazzling me with its

headlights. I lifted a hand in front of my eyes. Didn't the stupid sods understand what was happening?

'Where are we?' It was the guy on the cellphone. 'For the ambulance. Where are we?'

I started to answer, but my tongue felt heavy and clotted, and Ash beat me to it. 'Lithgow Street. Just round the corner from Pascoe Avenue.' The guy nodded and spoke into his phone.

'They're on their way,' he said as he got out of the car. 'What happened? Is she bad?'

'She came straight out in front of us,' Vince said. Again I remembered him being an idiot, me taking my eyes off the road. I said nothing.

The guy from the car stood holding a big umbrella over the girl. Another couple of drivers had stopped, and people were coming out of their houses. I heard voices. 'What's going on? . . . Some girl got hurt.'

I made myself move again. I strode over to where the girl lay sprawled, and knelt beside her once more. The guy with the umbrella said something, but I took no notice. I stretched out a hand, then pulled it back. I sucked in a breath, reached out a second time, and rested two fingers on the side of her neck, beside the jaw, like they'd taught us in First Aid at *Tae Kwan Do*.

Her skin was still warm. There hadn't been enough time to . . .

Then my body jerked as if someone had shoved me. I made a grunting noise, tried to hold myself still, felt again. Under my fingers a pulse flickered, ragged and feeble but there. She was alive.

I lifted my face into the rain. 'Come on!' I bawled. 'Come on!'

An impact severe enough to cause brain injury through tearing of tissues and nerve connections may also damage other organs. The violent movement may result in contusion (bruising) of the heart in its chest cavity. Kidneys and liver may suffer harm as well.

RYAN:

On the footpath, a woman from one of the houses was gabbling on. 'Ooh, it's awful the way some of them tear along here. I always knew something would happen.'

I wanted to scream and swear at her. Instead I yelled, 'Get a blanket! Go on – get a blanket!' She stared at me, and went.

Vince and Ash stood together, silent. The girl hadn't moved or made a sound. I saw that one of her sneakers was missing. But she was breathing. And there wasn't much blood. She might just be knocked out. It might be all right.

I knelt beside her once more, hugging myself and mumbling. I was soaked with rain now. A siren grew behind me, and an ambulance swung round the corner, blue lights flashing on the wet road. It pulled in behind the *Subaru*, and two figures jumped out. A man and woman, moving fast but calm. I stumbled towards them.

'Who's hurt?' the woman asked. Her eyes scanned me, Vince, Ash.

At first I couldn't speak. I blurted, 'Girl. There.' and pointed. They set off at a jog to where the guy stood with the umbrella. The ambulance man carried a plastic box.

COMING BACK

They squatted down beside the silent shape on the
road. After a moment, they looked at each other. The
moment I saw that look, I knew it wasn't going to be
all right.

CHAPTER THREE

RYAN:
The ambulance woman hurried to where they were parked, and came back with something like a fat plaster cast. They began fitting it carefully round the girl's neck. For a second, I had this sick thought that her neck must be broken. Then I remembered our *TKD* First Aid training again. You always immobilised the head of an injured person, to stop any spinal damage.

The ambulance guy shone a little torch, and I glimpsed her face once more. Neat nose, soft skin, eyes closed. The guy lifted one eyelid and aimed the torch. I saw the eye staring blankly back at him, and for a moment I thought I was going to spew.

'Minimal pupil response,' the ambulance man muttered. He glanced up at us. 'You know her name?'

I said nothing; my tongue felt thick and swollen again. Vince shook his head. Then Ash spoke. 'Tara.' We stared at him. 'She's in the same netball team as this girl I know. Tara somebody.'

Straightaway, both the ambulance crew began talking loudly to her. 'Tara! Can you hear us? Tara!'

No sound. No movement. Come on, I thought. Come on, please! 'She's got a pulse,' I said. It sounded stupid. The ambulance woman looked at me, then looked away. 'Tara!' she went again. The girl lay still.

The guy reached into his box and held a plastic oxygen mask over her – Tara's – face. With his other hand, he began pressing a rubber bulb. Suddenly I couldn't watch any longer. I turned, and banged into Vince. I shoved him aside, and stumbled away, my guts churning.

Another ambulance was arriving, siren wailing. No – red and blue lights this time. Cops.

It was another man and woman team. They went straight to the ambulance crew, who were kneeling under the umbrella that the guy with the cellphone still held over the girl. After a moment, he pointed to us three. The male cop came towards us; the woman began waving traffic on. The rain was lighter now.

'Who was driving, guys?' The cop was young and fair-haired.

I made a sort of mumble. 'See your licence?' he asked. I passed it over, knowing what was coming.

He looked at it, then at me. 'Restricted. Anyone with you?'

I could lie easily. Vince wanted me to; I could feel it coming from him. They could say they'd arrived after it happened. There were no witnesses except the girl, and she –

But . . . 'These two,' I said.

Vince made a hissing noise. Ash said, 'We asked –' but I stopped him. 'I said I would.'

There was no expression on the cop's face. 'We'll sort all that out later.' He nodded at my licence that he was holding. 'You still at this address?'

I didn't answer. The ambulance crew had the girl on a stretcher, mask still over her face, and were carrying her away. 'Taking her to Central?' the cop asked. The ambulance guy nodded.

'Can I go with her?' I blurted. The ambulance crew stared at me, then the woman shook her head. 'They'll want you here.'

They loaded the silent figure into the back and were off, siren lifting again. The male cop was by the *Subaru* now, looking at the shattered windscreen, peering inside. He stepped over to his car, then came back with something in his hand. 'You been drinking, Ryan?'

'No!' It came out harsh.

He held up something like a long flat cellphone. 'Say your name and address into this, please.'

My breath jerked as I spoke. My back and legs were shuddering. The cop looked at a little window on the side of what he was holding, then showed it to me. PASS, read the window. He put the cellphone thing away. 'OK.' His voice sounded a bit friendlier.

The guy with the umbrella stood beside us. 'Mind if I go now? My family will be wondering what's happened.'

So will mine, I thought. I pictured Mum and Jon. Then a movement made me look towards the footpath. More people had been arriving. Now a man and a woman came hurrying towards us, almost running. They stopped, talking loudly to others, asking something. I couldn't hear the words.

The woman stooped and snatched something from the gutter. In the streetlight, I saw a sneaker. 'It's Tara's!' she went. 'Tara!' She began rushing into the road, towards where the cop stood talking to me. The man grabbed and held her. Nobody needed to tell me who they were.

TARA:

Something gripped my head and neck. It was like the time Mel and Brittany sat on me when we were mucking about at a Year 7 Camp. I felt one of them blowing air into my face, and they were calling 'Tara! Tara!' Sod off and let me sleep, I wanted to say. But I was asleep already.

RYAN:

The cop began talking to the girl's parents. 'Where?' they kept asking. 'Where?' I heard the cop say 'Central. We'll take you'. The woman shook her head. 'No. No, we'll go ourselves.'

They didn't even glance my way. I don't know what I'd have done if they did. But, as they started off, the girl's father turned and stared at Ash and Vince and me, then went on after his wife. I never want anyone else to look at me that way for the rest of my bloody life.

On the Glasgow Coma Scale, unconscious patients are rated 1-5 in terms of their: (a) ability to open their eyes; (b) response to light and sound; (c) response to pain stimuli, e.g. pinching. A rating of 5 indicates clear response and near-consciousness. A rating of 1 indicates no response and deep unconsciousness. The patient's rating upon admission was 1 in each category.

Immediate treatment included shaving off the patient's hair above one temple, cutting a three-sided hole in her skull, and lifting up the resulting flap of bone to ease any intra-cranial pressure (brain swelling) resulting from her injury.

RYAN:

Another cop car arrived. The guy in it took over directing traffic from the policewoman. Most people were leaving – the show was over. The guy with the umbrella and cellphone had gone.

The cops from the first car came over to us. Rain glistened on their parkas. I realised again how soaked I was. My jacket had gone with her – Tara.

'All right, Ryan,' the fair-haired cop said. 'Someone will contact you.'

I wasn't hearing him properly. 'Can I drive the car?' I asked. 'I'll be careful.'

He must have thought I was being smart. He glared at me, then he seemed to see how I was. 'The car stays here. We'll want it for tests.' He kept watching me. 'You sure you're still at the same address?'

I was too gutted to answer. I just nodded. Traffic was back to normal now, and the other cop jerked a thumb towards his car. Vince and Ash sat silent in the back; I sat silent in the front. The cop didn't say anything either; the only sound was a few crackles on the car radio.

'I'm coming in with you,' Ash said when we got out at our place. Vince hesitated, then muttered, 'Yeah.' The cop watched as we trudged up the path to the front door.

Mum was in the hallway. She stared at us as we trooped in, sodden and hunched. 'Ryan, what . . ?'

Jon appeared behind her. 'Where's the car?'

26

I wanted to yell at him. Never mind the bloody car! When I spoke, my voice still sounded clotted and clumsy. 'The cops have got it. There's . . . an accident.'

My mother's breath jerked. Jon put his hands on her shoulders. 'I'm – we're all right,' I said.

We went through and sat in the dining room and I told them. Ash helped out. Vince mumbled a few things. My mother listened and gripped Jon's hand.

'The girl?' Mum asked when I'd finished. I shook my head. I'd been staring at the table while I talked and I couldn't look up now.

Vince rang his old man. 'I can't give you a lift home, sorry,' said Jon. His voice was flat. After maybe five minutes, a car arrived outside. Vince's father runs a car yard, so he's always driving some flash new wheels. 'See ya, mate,' Ash said. Vince muttered, 'Yeah. See ya.' He didn't look at me; I wondered what was going through his mind.

Mum wanted me to eat something or have a hot shower. I couldn't. So we just sat while another ten or fifteen minutes dragged by. 'The *Subaru*'s OK,' I said once. 'It's just the windscreen.' Jon nodded.

Finally I went to my room. I took off my wet T-shirt and my sneakers. I sat on the bed and stared at the posters on my wall. What was happening to the girl now? Was she –?

Then I was on my feet, smashing *TKD* kicks and punches at the door, howling and yelling, watching the skin on my knuckles tear and the blood start to run.

Out in the hall, Mum started yelling too. 'Ryan! No, love! Stop!' The door flung open and Jon charged in. He grabbed me and shook me so hard that the shock of it stopped me dead. 'It's no good, mate,' he panted. 'It's not going to help anybody.'

He was wrong. It had helped stop me from going bloody mad. I let Mum give me a pill. Then another pill. I lay curled under the bedclothes, like a little kid hiding. I heard someone blubbering, and knew it was me. After a while, I half-slept.

CHAPTER FOUR

In the case of a closed-head injury (where the brain is not exposed), the head should be kept immobilised till X-Rays show whether there is any spinal damage. If the patient seems unable to breathe or swallow properly, a ventilation tube must be inserted into the mouth. This was done.

The patient's reaction to light was tested hourly. Her pupils reacted sluggishly. The left lung had collapsed, punctured by a broken rib, and there was danger of the chest cavity filling with air, thus pushing other organs out of position. So a chest drain was inserted to relieve pressure.

TARA:
Lights kept shining. Someone was pressing on me and trying to stick things in my mouth. I hadn't got pissed at a party, had I? Mel and Brittany and I had promised we wouldn't let that happen to us. I couldn't tell. I couldn't remember things. My side still hurt. I was standing on a tiny island in the middle of a huge, slow river, and the river was eating the island away, bit by bit.

RYAN:
Mum made me eat some toast and stuff. I'd got up

29

about half-six. Hell, I never get up on school mornings till nearly eight.

The pills had knocked me out for a few hours. Then I lay and stared at the ceiling, hearing a car go up the street, breaking into a sweat when it sounded as if it was stopping outside our place, feeling like the world had started flying apart all around me. I heard other things, too: Mum crying and Jon murmuring to her.

I must have slept then, because, suddenly, I was driving the *Subaru* along a narrow road like a trench, with high concrete walls on either side. Someone was trying to get out of my way, but they couldn't climb the walls. I kept stabbing my foot at the brake, but there were weights or something holding my foot down, and the car just went faster and faster. I woke up with my heart banging, and my mouth stretched wide to yell. I sat on the edge of my bed after that till grey light started showing through the curtain.

Bits of last night whirled in my head. Me grabbing the DVD from Vince. The girl in the headlights. God, why hadn't she . . . ? Why me? I kept thinking. Why me?

Mum looked awful. The moment I came into the kitchen, she hugged me and kept holding me. Suddenly I ached to be a little kid again. I sucked in a big, shaky breath. 'We love you, son,' Mum said. 'We love you and we'll be with you.'

Jon was in the shower. 'OK, mate,' he said when he joined us at the table. 'Can we talk about a few things?' He didn't look like he'd slept either.

I didn't want to talk about anything. I didn't want to know about anything. I sat there and ate a piece of toast that I couldn't taste.

'I've rung Central Hospital,' Jon went on after a minute. The toast clogged in my mouth as I stared at him. My stepfather shook his head. 'They won't tell me how she is. Privacy Act. But she's alive, Ryan.'

I'd been holding my breath, chest locked. 'How –?'

'I rang the police, too. Told them who I was, why I was ringing. Her name's Tara Gower, by the way. The woman at the police station said the hospital would ring them if – if anything happened. It means the charges against you would change, mate.'

Mum gave a sob. I kept staring at Jon. I knew what he meant. I'd thought about it in the night, but I'd managed to keep the words away. Murder. Manslaughter.

Jon glanced at Mum, then back at me. 'We should have the car back in a couple of days. They're checking it for roadworthiness and . . . evidence. Pio from work is lending me his old banger till then.'

Mum held Jon's hand. 'You'll have to go to court, love. You know that.'

I nodded. I'd swallowed the toast, but my throat still felt blocked.

'We're with you, mate,' Jon said. 'We're not going to make excuses, but we're with you.' He paused. 'What do you wanna do?'

I had to punish myself. Hurt myself. If I kept doing that, then other people might not blame me so much. 'I want to go to the hospital.'

Closed-head injuries often cause swelling of brain tissue. There is then a danger of the cerebro-spinal fluid being compressed, and – in extreme cases – of brain tissue being squeezed down into the top of the spinal column, with fatal results.

An intra-cranial monitor was inserted in the patient's skull to monitor any signs of such swelling. To help blood drainage, her bed head was raised thirty degrees.

The chest drain appeared to be functioning. There was no indication of pressure build-up in the chest cavity.

RYAN:

Mum didn't like it. 'Why, love? They won't want you there.'

'I've got to.' I couldn't explain. Jon shook his head.

Mum sighed. 'I'll ring school and tell them you'll be away. Go and have a shower then eat some breakfast. You have to eat!' she told me as I started saying something. I'd only been going to say, 'Yeah'.

The hot water stung my knuckles, and I stared at the torn skin. I'd almost forgotten that business with my door. I put some plasters on. My door looked like it could do with a few plasters, too.

The phone rang as I came out of my room, and my guts turned to cold water. I stood still while Mum answered. When she said, 'Hello, Ash. Yes, I'll get him.' I had to stay for a second with one hand against the wall before I could move.

Ash's voice was quiet. 'Hi, mate. Just ringing to see how you are.'

I told him what Jon had found out from the cops. 'That's positive, mate,' Ash said. 'Mum reckons every hour improves their chances in this sort of thing. She's a netballer, remember, so she's fit. That helps. Oh – her name's Tara Gower.'

'I know.' I was remembering other things: the startled eyes as she stared at us; the sound of her head hitting. I clenched my teeth and squeezed the phone.

'Anything I can do?' Ash asked. 'You heard from Vince?'

No, I said. There was nothing he could do. And no, I hadn't heard from my best mate.

TARA:

The thing in my mouth was still there. I couldn't feel the rest of my head or body, but the thing was there, trying to push down my throat. I was too tired to fight it. All around me, the river kept eating away eating away at the island.

RYAN:

Jon drove me to Central Hospital. Pio's car was a banger, all right – a clapped-out *Holden* with bottles on the floor and tools on the back seat. 'I'll clean it out later,' Jon said. 'No, I'll do it,' I told him. He glanced at me, then nodded.

We found a place in the main car park. 'She'll be in Intensive Care,' Jon told me. 'You want me to come?'

Yeah, I did. I was scared shitless. 'Nah,' I said.

The hospital was four big square buildings in depressing grey concrete, about six storeys high. I found the main entrance. Inside was a shop selling flowers, chocolates, magazines, all kinds of brightly coloured stuff, and an Enquiries counter with a board listing wards and departments. Nothing about Intensive Care. I asked the woman behind the counter, who nodded at the board. 'Third Floor.'

I looked again. I.C.U. Sounded like a kid's joke. I walked down the shoe-squeaky corridor. Round the corner, they were pushing an old woman on a bed into a lift. Wild eyes stared from under white hair. I suddenly wondered – did the people here know who I was, what I'd done? What would I do if one of her friends or somebody had a go at me?

I climbed the stairs to I.C.U. It took longer that way. I came out opposite another counter, with chairs and a couple of low tables nearby. The woman here smiled at me. 'Can I help you?'

'Uh – Tara Gower. I was . . . '

She ran her finger down a list. 'Are you family or a friend?'

Oh shit. 'I –' Then a phone on the counter rang. 'I.C.U.,' the woman said. 'Valerie speaking.' To me she whispered, 'Doctor's with her now. Like to sit over there?'

I sat by one of the tables. A little way down the corridor were double doors with one of those touch-pad locks on the wall beside them. INTENSIVE CARE UNIT: NO UNAUTHORISED ADMISSION read a notice. She was on the other side of those doors.

I picked up a magazine, stared at it without seeing it, put it down again. The woman at the counter finished on the phone, typed something on a screen, went away down another corridor, came back and typed some more.

Five minutes passed. Ten. Fifteen. I had to find someone. I started to stand.

A man came out through the double doors of the Intensive Care Unit. Not a doctor: a guy in khaki pants

34

and a green jersey. My back cramped. It was the guy who'd looked back at me last night: Tara's father.

He was tall and bony, with glasses. His clothes were rumpled; you could tell he hadn't slept all night.

He hadn't looked at me. He wasn't really seeing anything. I heard him ask the Valerie woman if there was a public cafeteria in the hospital. She was nodding and telling him, her voice full of sympathy.

I'd kept my head down, but now I glanced up and the woman noticed me. 'Oh, there's someone else here asking about Tara.'

I sat like stone as the guy turned. He was so shattered, it took him a moment to even see me. Then he knew. His face changed suddenly, and he began walking towards me.

My body wouldn't move. Once again that feeling came of things breaking apart all around me. Then I stood, to face what was coming.

CHAPTER FIVE

RYAN:
He stopped in front of me. He had brown eyes like the girl's, but his were red and swollen at the corners. He looked at me for a moment, then his right hand came up.

My whole body flinched. He was going to whack me. But instead he took off his glasses and rubbed his face. 'You're the driver?'

I couldn't trust my voice. I nodded.

'What's your name, son?' I hate people calling me 'son', but this guy could call me anything he wanted. 'Ryan O'Carroll.'

He flopped down in the chair, as if all the strength had suddenly drained out of him. I slowly sat, too. 'I'm really sorry.' My voice sounded thick.

Her father just nodded. I made myself speak again. 'How is . . . she?' I couldn't say her name aloud. I didn't have the right to.

He sighed. 'I don't know. Nobody knows. She can't talk or move, and they don't know if she can hear us. She's having a CT scan – a brain scan – soon. Her mother's with her.'

'We weren't boozed,' I told him. 'I wasn't watching

properly, but we weren't boozed.'

He looked up at me then. It was the look I'd been scared of getting, and I felt my guts go heavy again. 'What did you come here for?'

I stared at the floor. 'I had to.'

There was silence for maybe five seconds. I knew he was watching me. 'OK, son,' he said finally. 'You better go now. I don't want Tara's Mum to see you. She's not really with it just now.' He paused, and his eyes went angry suddenly. 'I don't much want to talk to you, either.'

I stood. My legs felt heavy and clumsy. The woman at the counter smiled at me. She wouldn't if she knew.

The girl's father spoke. 'What's your last name again?'

He was still in the chair. 'O'Carroll,' I said. He just nodded.

Out in the car park, Jon had his head back on the seat and his eyes closed. I left him to it for a few minutes and wandered around the parked cars. Why me? I kept thinking again. Why me? Vince was the one who'd been sodding around, plus she'd come out so suddenly on to the road. It wasn't bloody fair if everyone was blaming me.

I kicked a stone so hard, it flew through the air and whanged off a flash red sports job parked near the exit. Nobody was in it; I couldn't have given a stuff if they were. After a few more minutes, I went back to our car.

Testing of pupil response to light continued hourly. A CT scan was made to identify damaged areas. It was agreed that an ECG (electro-cardiogram test) would be carried out if there was any indication the heart had been damaged by the accident impact.

Sixteen hours after admission, the patient began showing signs of arrhythmia – irregular heartbeat. This was attributed to a paralysing drug being used to prevent movements that might cause spiking (sudden blood pressure rises inside the brain). The drug was discontinued, and close monitoring of her heart functions continued.

RYAN:

I cleared up Pio's car when we got home. I stuck the bottles in our rubbish, and tidied the tools away into the boot. I vacuumed most of the gunge off the floor, and washed the outside. Anything to take my mind off what might be happening at the hospital. Jon said, 'Thanks, mate.' and headed off to check in at work. He can't afford time away; he and Mum are still paying off all sorts of bills.

I was winding up the hose when the phone rang inside. I stood there, not moving, till Mum came out on the porch. 'It's the police, love.'

Oh shit no. Please, no. But Mum was already saying, 'It's not that, Ryan. It's not that.' She tried a wobbly smile. 'They need you to come in and make a full statement; add anything to what you said last night.'

She came over and put her arms around me. The hose dripped on my sneakers. 'You're allowed to have someone there, since you're not seventeen yet. I'm coming with you.'

We had to take a taxi into town. I saw Mum hand

over twenty dollars to the driver; I was costing her in all sorts of ways. We walked into a brown-floored foyer, where a scruffy guy leaned on the counter, going 'Nobody told me I had to, eh? Nobody told me!'

The policewoman he was talking to was the one from last night. She saw us, went 'Just wait a minute, Reg.' and said 'Mrs O'Carroll? If you'd like to take a seat, Sergeant Bramling will be with you.'

Mum's chin was up and her mouth tight. We'd hardly sat down when a door opened and another cop appeared. 'You folks like to come through here?'

He led us down a corridor and into a small bare room. Green plaster walls, wooden table, three school-type chairs. 'I'm Karl Bramling,' he said. He shook hands with Mum, which I could tell she hadn't expected. 'Make yourselves comfortable – if you can on these chairs.'

He was middle-aged and going bald. Except for the uniform with a couple of medal ribbons on it, he looked like a schoolteacher. 'How're you feeling, Ryan? Managed any sleep?'

I hadn't been expecting that, either. I mumbled something.

He sat opposite us. The table had names and graffiti on it. WEST SIDE . . . HOMIES SUX. The cop – the sergeant – set two printed forms down in front of him.

'Now, folks.' His voice was calm, in control. 'The purpose of this visit is so we can get a formal statement from Ryan to add to last night's report from the officer at the scene.' He nodded at one of the forms, already covered in handwriting. 'Mrs O'Carroll, you're welcome to ask anything. Ryan,' he looked at me 'anything you say will be taken down and may be used in evidence. You understand that?'

I understood it, and it scared the crap out of me. The sentence about 'anything you say . . . ' sounded so pathetic in movies, but not now.

For the next half-hour he took me over what had happened last night – Christ, only last night – checking the other cop's report, writing on the second form, asking me question after question. Mum sat, gripping her bag.

Why did I have the car? 'I asked him to go to the supermarket,' Mum said quickly. It wasn't totally true. The sergeant nodded and wrote it down.

Had I driven anywhere else? I told him about *Video Ezy*. And where were Ash and . . . Vince, was it? . . . sitting when we started driving home? Were they fooling about or anything?

Yeah, I thought. Where was my best mate, anyway? Why hadn't he been in touch? He was the one who should be here. I tried to pull my head together as the cop started talking again.

'Remember we're after the full picture,' he said. 'We're not trying to blame your friends, but perhaps they distracted you without meaning to?'

Suddenly, I felt so shattered that I just couldn't be bothered. 'It was my fault,' I said. Mum went 'Ryan –' and I shook my head at her. The cop watched, and I knew he was missing nothing.

'Did you see the girl before the car hit her?'

I couldn't speak for a moment. Her face was there again, hair swinging as she turned to stare at us. 'Ash yelled out. I turned round and she – she was right in front.'

Mum squeezed my hand. The sergeant kept writing. We went on through my braking, the search for the girl, stopping the guy with the cellphone, the ambulance. When we finished, I was cold and shivering, but the feeling of things flying apart had faded a bit.

I read the statement through and tried to believe it was about me. I signed it; so did Mum.

'OK,' the sergeant said. 'Now, Ryan, there are two separate offences we're looking at here. You've admitted carrying passengers on a Restricted Licence, so you'll be sent an Infringement Notice for that. There's a fine – usually about $400, and you'll get demerit points on your licence. You can pay the fine at a bank, by the way.'

I snorted. I couldn't help it. The cop gave me a half-grin. 'Bit weird, isn't it?'

'Sergeant Bramling?' Mum's voice was tight. 'What about charges over the . . . the accident?'

The cop gazed down at his forms. 'We have to wait, Mrs O'Carroll. It depends on what happens to Tara.'

The pokey little room was silent. Outside, feet moved along the corridor. Someone laughed in another room. In another world.

The sergeant looked at me, and I thought of a schoolteacher again. 'Try to go on with things normally, Ryan. You got any sports or hobbies?'

'*Tae Kwan Do.*'

He nodded. 'Put some time into that. Keep yourself occupied. It's not going to help if we end up with two casualties.'

Mum thanked him. So did I, listening to my voice sound like someone else's.

We caught a bus home. Mum made me drink a cup of coffee and eat half a sandwich. Then I went out and walked around the streets till it was nearly 3.20 pm, and I turned for home in case I met anyone I knew coming out of school. Friday afternoon, I realised. Best time of the week: school over; the weekend ahead. Mates to hang out with, DVDs to watch, chicks to talk about, even wheels to drive.

But not this Friday. Maybe never any Friday again.

CHAPTER SIX

RYAN:

Ash rang half an hour after I got home. Tara was just the same. The girl Ash knew from her netball team and another friend had been to the hospital to see her. I didn't tell him how I'd gone there too, and how I'd met Tara's father. I was too busy thinking: Shit, what if I'd run into her friends there?

'No news is good news in something like this, love,' Mum told me. 'It really is.'

'Yeah, I know,' I said. And I did, but not the way she meant it. No news was ever going to be good for me now.

Since the patient had suffered such a severe impact, regular blood and urine tests were made to check the state of her kidneys.

There was concern at the possibility of sudden seizures or fits. These are a grave danger to closed head injury patients, as they increase the brain's demand for oxygen while actually reducing the supply.

Very gentle physiotherapy, focusing on chest and side massage, was begun.

TARA:

Darkness. Heat somewhere . . . in my head? But darkness silent and slow, and growing all around.

RYAN:

Ash rang again, before tea. He didn't really have anything more to tell me.

'Listen,' he went after a bit. 'Don't mean to sound like a bloody animal. But do you want to come round and watch those DVDs with Vince and me?'

Vince, I thought. I hesitated, then I shook my head. 'No. Thanks mate, but no.'

Mum must have guessed what we were talking about. 'You should go, Ryan. Staying home won't help.'

I just shook my head again. 'Where's your jacket?' my mother asked then. 'I couldn't find it with your other wet things.'

My jacket. I'd forgotten it. I remembered spreading it over the girl. I remembered her mother, holding the sneaker and screaming. 'It went with – with her,' I mumbled. 'To the hospital.'

Mum just nodded. 'Doesn't matter, love. Doesn't matter.'

I wanted to ring the hospital, but Mum said it was no use – they wouldn't give out patient details over the phone. Jon said the same as her, about no news being good news. 'Every hour helps, mate.'

Shut it, I wanted to tell them both. Just shut it and – and leave me alone. Everybody bloody leave me alone. I got up and walked out of the room.

Less than twenty-four hours after I'd maybe killed a girl, I went to bed. I didn't want to; I was frightened of what I might dream. But if I had any dreams on that Friday night, I don't remember them.

Since there was no evidence of stomach damage, high-calorie naso-gastric feeding was begun on the second day. Care was taken to avoid any infection of nasal or throat passages, in case breathing difficulties developed.

TARA:

There was something up my nose. Hey, you're really getting up my nose, I wanted to tell Brittany and . . . I couldn't remember my other friend's name.

RYAN:

Saturday morning. I tried to imagine what was happening at the hospital. Nobody had rung. Did that mean no change?

That cop – the sergeant yesterday – was right. I had to go on with things. I had to focus, like *Tae Kwan Do* teaches you. Jon was at work again, making up the time he'd missed on Friday, so I told Mum, 'I'll do some *TKD* this morning, then work on school assignments this afternoon.' She nodded; her eyes were tired and raw.

'Look after yourself, love,' she said, and hugged me. That just about started me howling again.

I've got a padded punching bag that hangs from a post Jon put up beside the garage. I did ten minutes stretching and loosening up, then I poured myself into kicks and punches at the bag. Roundhouse kicks, front kicks, spinning reverse kicks. My chest heaved and my muscles burned. I had to suffer. I had to be hurt too, just like Tara was. Finally, I slumped on the concrete, head between my knees, dragging in breath while the world kept spinning around me.

The phone shrilled inside the house, and my back went cold. How long till I could hear a phone without being terrified? The back door opened, and I kept staring at the concrete. 'It's Ash, love,' Mum called. I heard my breathing start again.

'Hi, mate. How's it goin'?' Those five words are about as much as Ash usually speaks in a whole day. By his standards, he'd been gabbling since Thursday night.

We talked for a while about nothing much. I wanted to ask if the girl he knew had been to the hospital again, but I was too scared. Then he said, 'Vince is here,' and my best mate came on the line.

Vince is a talker – he's the one who chats up the chicks when we're out together. But he was struggling today. After a bit, he ran out of things to say. 'You coming round?' he went.

'Nah. Got some stuff I'd better do.' I could hear the relief in Vince's voice as he said, 'See ya, then,' and hung up. I stood there for a few seconds. Didn't he bloody understand what I was going through? When was he going to face up to what he'd done? I began to stab at the phone. I'd tell him . . . Then I stopped.

Jon came home at lunchtime. 'Pio didn't even recognise his car, mate.' He and Mum sat on at the table after we'd eaten, drinking coffee and talking. They hadn't got a Saturday paper, I realised. They usually read the Saturday paper after breakfast and lunch. I could guess why they hadn't got it this weekend; I wondered how many kids at school knew what had happened, what they were saying about me.

I did a couple of hours' work on an Information Technology assignment I'd usually have whizzed through in half an hour, then I sat staring out at the garden. Jon and Mum were there, bent over some shrubs that needed cutting back. Most Saturdays I'd be down at Southside Plaza by now, pigging out on *McD's*, watching the chicks with Vince and Ash. I wondered if they'd gone there.

But mostly I wondered about the girl. I sat there, trying to imagine it, clenching my fists till my fingernails stabbed into my palms. She was still the same. She was gonna be a cripple (I kept seeing that neck brace). She was gonna be a vegeta – but I still couldn't even think that. My head jerked back and my eyes screwed shut if I pictured it. The other possibility, that she was better, was something I couldn't think about, either.

The phone went again. And when I made my body move to get to it, a voice I didn't recognise for a second said he was Richard Gower, Tara's father, and four hours ago, his daughter's heart had stopped.

CHAPTER SEVEN

RYAN:

I'll never forget it. For the rest of my life, I'll never forget it. Outside, the Saturday sun stroked the garden. My mother said something to my stepfather and gave him a tired smile. And on the phone, this guy described how his sixteen-year-old daughter's heart had stopped.

He hadn't meant to phone me. *Victim Support* were the ones who looked after this sort of thing. But he'd rung – he'd rung about my bloody jacket. There was this black and silver one with Tara's things. He'd been going to give it to the hospital people to pass on to the cops. Then he'd wondered if maybe it was mine. I said it was. Then I swallowed and asked, 'How is she?'

His words came out clotted, like someone else was speaking through his mouth. 'She had a severe cardiac arrhythmia – her heartbeat got so irregular, it started to shut down. About twelve o'clock.'

My arms and legs spasmed. My eyes bulged and my mouth stretched. I jerked the phone away as if it had clawed me. Oh shit, no! someone inside my head was gasping. OH SHIT, NO!

TARA:

Something paused. It was like a big engine you've got so used to, you never notice it working. Then it switches off, and whispers into silence. I drifted high above emptiness. Then very gently, I began to fall.

RYAN:

On the phone, her father's voice kept coming. She was alive. The monitors on the I.C.U. machines had started beeping. The nurses were there in five seconds to give her resuscitation, and she'd responded straightaway.

I sat shuddering and gasping, the receiver in my hand. Mum stuck her head through the door. 'Ryan, have you seen –? Ryan, what's happened?'

She snatched the phone from me. 'Who is this? What's going on?' She listened while I hugged myself and tried to breathe properly. Then she said, 'Mr Gower, it's Kathryn O'Carroll – Ryan's mother. I'm . . . we're all so sorry. Please – I know we don't have any right, but can we talk to you sometime?'

I glanced up. Mum's face was pale. So were her knuckles where she gripped the phone. She spoke again.

'I understand. We don't want to cause any more hurt. But if we could just tell you face to face . . . ' Another pause, then, 'Yes. Yes. Thank you for listening.' She hung up, said, 'He's going to think about it', and put her arms around me. Jon came in then, stared at the two of us, and Mum told him what had happened. Afterwards, I made it to my room, and lay curled up in a ball on my bed. And just like that first night, I heard myself bawling.

Severe cardiac arrhythmia and resuscitation will cause blood pressure changes, which may damage the blood-brain barrier. The patient must be closely monitored, and probably sedated.

RYAN:
Later, Mum made me eat some dinner; then she and Jon sat me down and we watched a DVD. They hardly ever watch DVDs; they read, or else Mum studies for this Office Skills course she's doing. But tonight, we all watched, though I didn't really take anything in.

Usually on Saturday night I'd be out with Ash and Vince, talking about the parties we were going to crash, and never really getting past the talking. This Saturday, I was home with my folks and a DVD. If I could have spent Saturday nights like that forever, it would have been just fine by me.

A central venous line, inserted in the patient's arm to supply fluids, was continually checked, as was the saline drip that maintained her salt levels. Her head was kept aligned with the spine to prevent any twisting and spinal damage.

There were no further complications from the collapsed lung. The broken rib and the lung wound seemed to be healing. It was agreed that the lung drainage tube should remain in place as long as the patient was being ventilated.

RYAN:
I slept half the night. When I was little, Mum used to take me to a park (so she could get away from my father, I reckon). There was this statue of kids who

could fly, and I used to wish I could do that, too – just fly away and leave everything behind. I wished it again now.

About 4 am, I got up and stood by the window. The shrubs and lawn were black and silver in the moonlight. A darker patch of shadow moved, and next door's cat flowed over the side wall.

I pictured Central Hospital, where a girl lay while her body decided if she'd live or die. She couldn't die, not while so many people were willing her to live. She couldn't.

I squeezed my hands into fists, and begged her inside my head. 'Come on! Come on!'

TARA:

Time had passed: I don't know how much. There'd been a panic – something beeping, people hurrying, voices calling somewhere near or faraway. It was over now. I kept drifting, but I wasn't falling any more. Somehow I'd turned around.

RYAN:

I went to *Tae Kwan Do* on Sunday morning. We have it in a hall that the local Play Centre use, so there's all these little kids' art and stuff up around the walls, like explosions in a paint factory.

Nobody said anything about the accident. Greg the instructor never lets us talk, anyway. 'Mouth closed, mind open,' he says. We did speed work and pad work. The hall echoed with fists and feet whacking into pads, and voices yelling 'Haaa!' I felt some of the knots inside me loosen.

'Good, Ryan,' Greg said as we stretched and warmed down at the end. 'You OK for Tuesday?' I realised then that he knew; Greg never imagines that anyone might not come to a *TKD* practice. I said 'Yeah.', and realised too that for the first time, I was looking past the next couple of hours.

Back home, I told Mum I'd ring Ash. She was pleased. So was he: 'Hi, mate. Vince and I were planning to call you – see if you wanted to go down to *McD's*.'

So we went, the three of us. I was shit-scared people would look at me, or start whispering who I was. But nobody did. They just seemed to be getting on with their own lives.

I didn't eat much. Vince was pretty twitchy. 'What are you going to tell the cops?' he asked once. 'I already have,' I said, and he stared. I waited, but he didn't say any more. You bloody . . . I felt the words begin to swell in my throat. Then the same tiredness, the same I-just-can't-be-bothered feeling I'd had with the police sergeant swept over me again. 'I told them it was my fault.' Vince looked at the ground.

He seemed keen to get away after that, and Ash had already used up his week's ration of words. But I was glad I'd come . . . I suppose.

I worked on some Economics stuff I should have done a couple of weeks back. It was getting on for dinner time when I heard a car pull up. I went to the window, and there was this dark-blue hatchback I'd never seen before, parked in our drive with someone getting out.

'Mum,' I said. She joined me at the window, and I felt her go tense.

He'd shaved, but he still looked shattered. The skin of his face seemed loose, as if he'd lost weight suddenly. We stood watching for a second. Then Mum opened the door to Tara Gower's father.

CHAPTER EIGHT

In closed head injuries, damage may be progressive. Functions may continue for some days before problems appear. So constant checks of pupil reactions and intra-cranial blood pressure must be made.

Infection is another danger. The body's systems may not be receiving the appropriate brain messages to fight bacteria.

TARA:
I drifted slowly upwards. I was so tired, and there was so far to go. My throat felt sore.

RYAN:
Mum said something to Mr Gower. I don't know what; you could tell how scared she was. Jon came through from the living room; he and the girl's father looked at each other.

'You work at *Blaine's Auto-Electrical*,' Mr Gower said.

'Yeah. And you're the rep for *Trident Electronics*,' replied Jon.

Things were a bit easier after that. Mum asked him to come in. Tara's father hesitated. 'I can't stay. Sally – Tara's Mum – has just come home. The doctor's given her some sleeping pills.'

But he came through and sat down. 'Will you have a cup of tea?' Mum asked. 'Please?' she added, as he hesitated again. 'I'm sure you haven't been eating properly.'

She gave him tea and biscuits. '*Victim Support* have been to see us,' he said, and my stomach lurched at the word 'victim'. 'I told them what you'd asked –' he nodded to Mum. 'So, anyway, here I am.'

'I'm so sorry. We're all –' Mum stopped as she choked up.

Silence for a while. Jon said something about work. I didn't know what to say about anything. After a bit, Mum spoke again. 'We've got no right to intrude. We know that. But we're thinking of you all the time.'

He – Mr Gower – gazed down at his tea. Then Jon said, 'Ryan's a good kid, Richard.' (It took me a moment to realise who 'Richard' was.) 'We're not making any excuses for him, but he's a good kid.' I just gaped; I'd never heard Jon talk like that before.

Tara's father lifted his head. His voice was flat and angry. 'Maybe he is. But the best kid I know in the world is lying there in hospital. She's the only one who matters right now.'

He turned to me, and suddenly he looked shattered again. 'We've all driven like that, sometime. But you never will again, will you?' I managed to nod.

'You think you've kept them safe.' The guy seemed to be talking to himself. 'You teach them to swim and to buckle up. You tell them about stranger danger, and you make sure they have their injections. Then . . . ' All of us were silent once more.

When he left a few minutes later, Mum asked, 'Please let us know if anything happens.' He muttered something. He walked down the path without saying goodbye, and drove away.

When a patient breathes with ventilator assistance, there is a danger of fluid collecting in the lungs. This may lead to pneumonia and/or other complications. To prevent this, physiotherapy involving the patient's chest and abdomen was continued.

TARA:
Someone was shaking me. Really softly, along my side, like they didn't want anyone else to know. It wasn't time to get up or something, was it? My throat hurt.

RYAN:
I slept about the same on Sunday night. I had breakfast. Mum hugged me like I was a five-year-old starting Year 1, and I headed for school.

Ash was coming along the street as I turned the corner. It's miles off his usual way to school. No sign of Vince; neither of us mentioned him.

'She's just the same,' Ash told me before I could ask. 'Mel – she's the one I know – and Brittany went again last night.' I didn't know who Brittany was, and I didn't care.

Kids at school had heard, but nobody really said anything. I saw a couple of girls watching me and whispering. A few of my other mates asked, 'You OK?' Vince spent lunchtime hanging around with Ash and me, yakking about his CD collection and stuff. Half my mind listened to him. Half couldn't believe what I was hearing. He still wouldn't look me in the face.

I poured myself into my schoolwork. It helped keep my mind busy, plus it was like showing I could do things, not just mess them up.

Jon arrived home after work in the *Subaru*, with a new windscreen. 'It's fine, mate,' he said. 'Pio reckons it looks nearly as good as his heap now.' I looked at it, and never wanted to drive again.

There was a letter for me – an official-looking one. I knew what it was before I opened it. *Police Infringement Bureau . . . Carrying Unauthorised Passengers While Holding a Restricted Licence . . . Fined $400 . . . 25 demerit points.*

I had about $500 in my savings account – delivering circulars; birthday money; a week's work last holidays for Vince's old man in his car yard. Vince and I had been talking about buying a car together, sometime. Now – 'I'll pay it,' I told Mum. She just nodded. 'Good, Ryan.'

I remembered the court hearing that still lay weeks or even months ahead, and the sergeant talking about what the charge could be. The words rose in my mind again. Why me? Why me?

After her arrhythmia crisis the previous day, close monitoring of the patient's heart condition continued. There were no signs of associated problems.

Decisions had to be made on how much to move the patient in bed. Too much might cause pressure spiking in the brain. Too little might cause blood clots, decline in heart and lung functions.

RYAN:

I slept till about four again, and got up at six-thirty. Just over a hundred hours since the accident, and I still didn't know if she was going to live or die. Time crawled past. At home last night, I didn't check my watch till I knew two hours had gone. When I looked, it was just forty minutes.

At morning interval, I was heading for B Block when the two chicks I'd seen whispering yesterday came up to me. A dark one, and one from my English class, with messy blonde hair. 'You were driving the car when Tara Gower got hurt?' the blonde went.

I just looked at her. 'Her friends Mel and Brittany go to Girls' High with my cousin,' the dark one said. 'They're gonna give you shit, boy!'

'How is she?' I asked. They both stared at me. 'How should I know?' the dark chick said.

'I do,' I said. 'I know because I keep asking everyone who might bloody know.' The words sounded as if someone else was saying them.

The girls glanced at each other. 'So?' demanded the blonde.

'So piss off!' A voice spoke from beside me. Vince. The girls glared at him. 'Up yours!' one of them said, and they bounced off, muttering. Vince and I headed for B Block. He didn't say anything else, but for a bit, it was almost like things used to be, before.

TARA:

A long distance away, something kept thumping. A slow, quiet beat. I listened to hear if it would come again; instead I heard my own breathing. I can do this,

I thought. I felt . . . interested.

RYAN:

I went to *TKD* on Tuesday evening. Everyone knew now. Nobody said anything – maybe Greg had spoken to them – but a couple of the younger ones stared.

I spent most of the time teaching the juniors their basic punching patterns. I did it slowly, carefully. There's this kid about nine or ten called Sonja. I was holding her elbow while I showed her how to rotate her wrist. I looked at the bones in her skinny little arm, and I thought how incredible, how bloody incredible.

I came home and had a shower. I felt hungry. I actually felt hungry. I'd just got to the kitchen when the phone rang.

Mum answered while I stood still, hand on the cupboard. 'Yes,' I heard her saying. 'Yes, it is. Oh, hello . . . What? Is she? Oh, thank you! Thank you so much!'

Her voice cracked on the last words. I couldn't move my hand; it was still clamped round the cupboard door when my mother came into the kitchen. Her eyes were wild; her mouth quivered. We stood there, staring at each other.

'That was *Victim Support*,' Mum said finally. 'Mr Gower asked them to tell us that Tara's breathing almost normally. If there are no problems tonight, they're going to take her off the ventilator.'

I said nothing for a second. Then I went, 'Thank you,' like some total bloody wally. Mum started to speak, started to smile, and started to howl. I couldn't. Instead, I stood there like my whole body had been turned to concrete.

Three days ago, a phone call made me think she was dead. Tonight, a call made me believe she might recover. I had no idea how much, or what she'd be like in mind and body. But suddenly I knew I'd do anything I could to help. Anything. And I had to start by meeting her mother.

CHAPTER NINE

RYAN:

I told Jon so on Wednesday morning. I'd slept much the same: a few hours, then jolting awake with a car swerving under me, grabbing for controls I couldn't reach in time. I got up about half-six and went for a run. If anybody had seen me doing this a week ago, they'd have thought they were having the bad dream. Jon rubbed the bristles on his chin (he shaves maybe twice a week). 'You sure about this, mate?'

Of course I was bloody sure! What the hell did my stepfather know about what was going on in my head? I made myself answer as calmly as I could. 'I have to know – see if I can do anything.'

Jon nodded slowly. 'Let me square it with your Mum first.' We shut up as my mother came through. She was smiling, still on a high from last night's phone call, but her eyes were sunken. Yeah, Jon was right, I couldn't load any more stress on her just now.

Ash was waiting at the corner again. So was Vince this time. When I told them about her – Tara; I still can't say her name easily – coming off the ventilator, Ash went 'Awesome, mate!' Vince looked as if he'd had a year's detention cancelled. Nearly six days, and still no sign of him facing up to how much the accident was his fault. It was – if he hadn't been messing around with that DVD, then I wouldn't have . . . But somewhere inside me, I knew Vince wasn't going to say anything.

At interval, I passed the two chicks from yesterday. They took no notice of me, and I took no notice of them.

Six days after admission, with the patient breathing normally, the ventilator and lung drainage tubes were removed. A tracheotomy (insertion of a tube into an incision made in the throat) was carried out, to clear away mucus and help the patient breathe properly.

Later the same day, symptoms of fever appeared. There were discharges from nose and throat. Antibiotics were administered, and basic cooling care discussed.

TARA:
I felt hot again. Netball? No, must be the fish and chip shop. Hey, I knew a fish and chip shop! I wanted to tell someone, but I couldn't make a noise. I tried to swallow. My throat was still sore. It hurts, I wanted to tell someone. It hurts.

RYAN:
'Jon says you want to see Tara's mother,' Mum said when I got home on Wednesday. 'Leave it a couple more days, love? They'll only be able to handle so much. I keep trying to imagine what it's like for her. What it would be like for me, if you were . . . the one.'

'All right,' I said. 'I just want to tell her I'm sorry.'
Mum put her hand against my cheek. 'Don't punish

yourself too much, Ryan. You can get so wrapped up in hurting yourself, you forget what it's for. I was like that after your Dad and I broke up.'

My father. Mr Non-Event. I hadn't heard anything from him about the accident, surprise surprise. 'I'll be OK,' I told Mum.

I did some more *TKD* – high kicks against the punching bag. I worked hard, but I was careful, too. I was starting to realise that I had to start building something up, not just smash it down.

Polar air and cool cloths were applied to lower the patient's feverish temperature.

Insulin infusions to reduce rising blood sugar levels were begun through a tube into an arm vein. Excess blood sugar levels can cause organ damage and death in trauma patients.

RYAN:

I kept thinking of her all the time. I tried to remember properly what she looked like. Sounds pathetic, but I saw her only those moments in the half-dark.

Thursday morning on the way to school, Ash told me that whatsername . . . Mel and the other whatsername – Brittany – had been to see Tara again. She was off the ventilator, all right. I felt heaps better. 'But they're a bit worried she's getting a fever,' Ash said, which scared the shit out of me again.

'These chicks the other day –' I told him. 'They reckoned a couple of her friends want my guts.'

I half-expected him to laugh. Instead he went, 'Yeah, that'll be Brittany. She's a real wild woman. You want me to talk to her and Mel?'

'Yeah.' Then suddenly I knew. 'Actually, no. I want to talk to them.'

TARA:

Someone was pinching my leg. I tried to twitch away. Then they pinched my arm. Piss off! Leave me alone!

On Day Seven, the patient showed responses to painful stimuli. Her temperature was down, and the fever less. It was decided to end sedation, to allow tests that would measure the degree of brain damage.

The tracheotomy in the patient's throat was regularly checked, to ensure proper airway control.

RYAN:

Thursday evening came and went. A week. In the middle of the night, I had this godawful nightmare where I was trying to stop someone bleeding while they twisted around on the ground, but hands kept pulling me away. I woke up shuddering and gasping, and lay watching the ceiling grow out of darkness as day came.

I worked like hell all through Friday's lessons. I tried to, anyway, but my mind kept jumping ahead. Ash had told me that the two girls, Mel and Brittany, wanted to meet us at Southside Plaza after school. Tara's fever was down, Mel had said.

I saw the Girls' High uniforms on a seat outside the shops. Two of them; two of us. Vince had to do some car-waxing for his old man – he said.

Mel was dark and slim and really cute-looking. She gave me a half-smile. Brittany was shorter: fair hair and green eyes. No smile from her: she glared at me, then stood up. 'Come round here.' She strode off round the side of the car park building. Mel glanced at us, and followed. Ash and I trailed behind.

Brittany headed into a playground and lawn area where little kids raced around while their mothers watched. She plonked herself down on a bench. After a second, Mel sat beside her. We guys stood in front of them. The four of us probably looked like we were chatting one another up. A woman with a pushchair smiled at us. Then she saw Brittany's face, and stopped smiling.

'What's all this crap for?' Brittany demanded. 'We're supposed to come running if you whistle, are we?' Mel shot us another glance; she had long, dark eyelashes.

My face went hot. It was none of Brittany's bloody business. But I took two deep breaths, like at *TKD*, and told her, 'I just . . . I'm sorry.'

The green eyes kept glaring. 'Bit late, isn't it?'

I said nothing, but I looked straight back at her. The glare switched to Ash as he spoke.

'It wasn't just Ryan's fault, eh? There was . . . this mate who was mucking around. And she – Tara – came flying out on to the crossing. We never saw her coming.'

Brittany sneered. 'Yeah, yeah. I knew you guys would stick together.'

Hell, I didn't have to take this. 'What – like you chicks are sticking together now?'

For a moment, I thought she was going to jump up and whack me. Just let her try. I'd – Then dark-haired

Mel spoke. Her voice was quiet. 'The girls at school are making paper dolls to send Tara. There's hundreds of them. They've all got messages.'

'Sweet,' Ash went.

Brittany broke in. Her voice wasn't quiet. 'She could be a vegetable! They might have to feed her like a baby for the rest of her life. And you're talking about bloody paper dolls!'

A couple of little kids nearby had stopped playing and stood staring at her. Ash started to say something. So did Mel. My mate was keen on the dark-haired chick, I realised. She was cute, all right. But neither of them could stop Brittany.

'You guys are useless! Belting around in cars and thinking you're big men. Why don't you bloody grow up!'

She was going to howl. She jumped up, fair hair bouncing, snatched her arm away as Mel reached out a hand, and charged off. Mel gave us an embarrassed look, said, 'Sorry' to Ash, and hurried after her.

CHAPTER TEN

RYAN:
So yeah, it was another shitty Friday afternoon. I got wild on the way home – how would that Brittany chick feel if Ash and Vince started laying into her because their friend had gone running out onto the road? I was having to take all the crap.

Then I remembered Brittany almost bawling. And I thought of the other girl lying unconscious in hospital while we ate and walked and talked. Everything I'd been thinking seemed to shrink all of a sudden.

I did thirty minutes with the punch-bag, my spinning reverse kicks reaching higher and higher. Then Vince rang. He had been doing some job for his old man at the car yard, and he wanted to know if I'd like a couple of hours' work there tomorrow. I hesitated, then I said yeah.

Just before tea, *Victim Support* rang. 'Mr Gower asked us to tell you that Tara is no longer being sedated.'

For maybe three seconds, I thought they were pulling the plug on her, turning off life-support. I hunched over the phone. Then I realised the woman was telling me it was so the doctors could do more tests.

'So she's getting better?' I blurted. The voice at the other end was careful. 'I can't really comment on that.'

I slept on and off through Friday night. The ninth night since it happened. After breakfast on Saturday, Jon and Mum and I sat and tried to make sense of things. Mr Non-Event never did that; he was always flashing off somewhere. I suppose I've got to hand it to Jon.

We talked about school, and how getting stuck into my subjects helped. (Yeah, they'd noticed.) About *TKD*, and Ash and Vince, and working for Vince's dad. 'Might be able to get you a bit, too.' Jon said, rubbing his even-stubblier chin.

There was a pause. Mum and my stepfather glanced at each other. He gave her a nod. Mum hesitated, then turned to me.

'I found this magazine article on another girl who had a head injury,' she said. 'I don't know if you want to read it, love. It's pretty heavy. But it . . . it might help you understand what Tara could be facing.'

I took the magazine from her and held it like it might explode.

As sedation wore off, careful monitoring of the patient continued. Her heart, kidneys and blood pressure all seemed normal. Her pupils were checked regularly. Their unsedated response to light would be the first measure of any brain damage.

RYAN:

In my room, I read the article. This girl had sneaked out to a party, and her boyfriend crashed his car. Two years after she got out of hospital, she was still having headaches so bad, they made her sick. She couldn't smile properly or pronounce some words. She couldn't learn things the way she could before. She lost her temper for no reason. She was still having to see doctors, physios, counsellors, therapists.

When I'd finished, I just lay on my bed and felt tired. I wanted to help. But could I? Would it take the rest of my life? I didn't think I could handle this. There was a knock on my door, and Mum came in. She sat down beside me and held my hand. 'I'm sorry, love. Jon and I thought you should know.' She smoothed the hair back off my forehead, and I thought for a second I was going to bawl again. 'I'll ring tomorrow,' she said. 'I'll ask about you seeing Tara's mum then.'

TARA:
A brightness. No, just less darkness. Very far away, I could hear noises. Someone pinched me again. I opened one eye . . . or something opened it. More brightness, swimmy and blurry. I was somewhere different. Something had happened to me.

RYAN:
Vince and I spent Saturday afternoon washing cars in his father's yard. We hosed them down, vacuumed and waxed them, put paper mats on the floors, painted black stuff on the outside of the tyres. Vince kept looking as if he was going to say something, but he didn't. I wasn't going to make it easy for him, so we spent most of the time being a pair of Black Holes.

Again, I pictured the girl lying in hospital, not moving while I bent and turned. How much would I face up to, if it could make her all right? Would I stick my leg out and let a car run over it? Would I lie down and let . . . Ah, it was no good thinking that way.

I realised Vince was talking. 'You want to come round tonight? Ash and I got some more DVDs.'

I took a second to clear my head, then, 'OK,' I told him. Vince's whole face seemed to relax. He looked so pathetic, I nearly laughed out loud. Mr Cool, wagging his tail at me just so I'd go easy on him.

Anyway I went, which made Mum pleased. I had a couple of beers, my first since the accident. The three of us sat and watched. It was almost like normal, sometimes. We even laughed at a couple of the gross-out bits.

'That Brittany,' Ash said when we were leaving. 'You don't want to take any notice of her.' I shrugged. Vince wanted to know who Brittany was, of course; he always does when he hears about some new chick.

I walked home – I'm still not interested in driving. I slept maybe five hours. Then I stared at the ceiling and thought about the girl in that magazine article.

TARA:
Yeah, there was something different. I was different. How long . . . How much . . . I didn't even know what I wanted to ask. I couldn't put anything together. Something was missing.

RYAN:
Sunday morning at *TKD*, I coached the juniors again.

'That's great,' a guy who must have been little Sonja's father told me at the end. 'Really appreciate the trouble you take.' Greg gave me a nod, which is his way of saying 'Brilliant'.

When I got home, Mum said, 'I rang *Victim Support*, Ryan – about your wanting to see Tara's mother.'

A thrush was making little runs on the lawn, sticking its beak in the ground, darting off in a new direction. Mum put an arm around my shoulders. 'They phoned back and said the Gowers will be at the hospital all day. You can go this afternoon, if you want to.'

'Yeah,' I said. 'Thanks.' I didn't want to, but I had to.

I ate a bit of lunch. Nearly ten days. Getting on for 240 hours. How many hours and days would I give up from my life, if that could mean it had never happened?

I headed off for the hospital about two o'clock. 'Take the *Subaru*, mate,' Jon told me. I started to tell him not to be so bloody thick; that I never wanted to drive again. Instead, I drove so carefully to Central that two cars behind honked at me.

I followed the polish-smelling corridor and stairs up to I.C.U. The Valerie woman was behind the desk. 'I've come to see Tara Gower's mother,' I told her. She just nodded.

I sat on the same chair I'd sat on nine days before. I picked up the same magazine, something about fishing. I turned the pages and still didn't take in a word.

She came after just two minutes. I had the magazine open at the same, unread page. She was Mum's height;

short haircut that showed her ears. You could tell she'd been cute once. Now she was exhausted, and stretched tight, and totally unstoppable.

I stood up as she came towards me. Blue eyes – not her daughter's colour. Something I'd learned in Biology skidded stupidly into my mind. The brown eye gene is dominant over blue.

'Ryan?' she asked. I managed a nod. I waited for her to hit me, like I'd waited for her husband. Instead, she stood and just looked at me for a couple of seconds. Then she stepped forward and put her arms around me.

I thought I'd been ready for anything. Anything except that. Next second I'd flopped down in the chair. My hands were over my face, and once more I was blubbing and bawling like a little kid.

CHAPTER ELEVEN

RYAN:

She sat down next to me, and passed me a tissue. 'We've been using a lot of these.'

I blew my nose, and then I didn't know where to put the sodding tissue. I didn't know where to look, either. Over at the desk, Valerie was sorting through a folder. This sort of thing probably happened all the time in I.C.U. Shit, if Ash or Vince or anyone at school saw me like this . . .

I pulled in a shuddering breath, and dragged one hand across my eyes. 'I'm sorry.'

'I know you are,' the woman said. 'You've come here.'

'How – how is she?'

Tara's mother sighed. 'She's hanging in, Ryan.' A pause. 'Her breathing's OK now. Her temperature's down, and she's responding to being touched.'

Relief poured through me. It was so enormous, I actually felt my body swell. Yet I knew there was something else coming.

Her eyes were tired but steady. 'They still don't know how much brain damage she has. Now the sedation is wearing off, they'll start to find out.'

There it was. The fear that still made my eyes screw shut. Would I end up wishing she had died? I sucked in another breath. The tissue in my hand was soggy and disgusting, but I used it again.

More footsteps. Tara's father appeared. 'Mr Moore is here, Sally. He wants to talk to us.' He gave me a half-nod.

Mrs Gower stood. So did I. 'We have to go, Ryan,' her husband said. It was the first time he'd spoken my name. Tara's mother took his hand, hesitated a moment, then spoke to me. 'You can phone us at home, if you want.'

I nodded, though they were already moving away. Yeah, I'd phone. Because there was still one person I had to see. Tara.

Ten days after admission, the danger from brain spiking had receded. There was no sign of fits or seizures, though occasional spastic twitching in the legs occurred. The intra-cranial monitor was removed.

TARA:
Something pressed on my head. Then it went away. I wasn't drifting any longer. I was more . . . solid. But I didn't know where I was, what I was. Big gaps in everything.

RYAN:
I couldn't drive home straightaway. I sat in the *Subaru*, holding the steering wheel. It felt friendly and ordinary. My hands looked the same. The feeling swept over me again. If only I could just wish myself

into a time where none of this had ever happened. I drove home so slowly that three cars honked at me. Mum and Jon were in the garden again. I told them what Mrs Gower had said. 'We just wait, love,' Mum told me. 'That's all we can do.'

Ash had rung, so I phoned him back. 'You've been to the hospital?' he asked. 'How was it?' I mumbled something.

He'd been talking to Mel. She said Brittany knew she shouldn't have gone over the top like that, but she'd never admit it. 'Brittany never says she's sorry,' Ash told me.

I pictured the fair hair and glaring green eyes. Yeah, I bet she didn't.

I worked on a Print Media assignment for English during the afternoon. Words help, I was starting to realise. I did some *TKD* stretching exercises, but by half-nine, I felt as if someone had spent the day twisting my neck one way and my shoulders the other. So I went to bed.

It was the best sleep I'd had in the ten days. I didn't wake till the first grey-white light was colouring the curtains. Outside, the whole street was still. Then a single bird spoke four notes, and another bird spoke back. I'd never noticed things like that before. I tried to imagine Tara. What sort of sleep and waking was there for her?

Children and adolescents seem to recover better from brain injury than adults. This may partly be due to the fact that their brains are not yet 'hardwired', i.e. uninjured areas can take over functions normally performed by the injured parts.

At the same time, an adolescent has usually learned more than a younger child, so s/he may have a wider basis of understanding to start rebuilding on.

RYAN:

Monday lunchtime at school, those two chicks who'd said how Mel and Brittany were after me just walked past like they'd never seen me before. They weren't trying to put me down; I reckon they'd really forgotten me. People are so separate.

Eleven days after admission, with sedation almost worn off, examination of the patient's pupils confirmed an unevenness in size – L pupil 5 mm, R pupil 6 mm. This could indicate some other brain incident or damage.

TARA:

Light in my eyes. Yeah, someone's opening them. Can I do it, too? Is it Mum? Or is it . . . ? I keep forgetting my friends' names.

RYAN:

Ash and Vince were waiting at the corner again on Tuesday morning. Made me laugh, almost – the two of them looked like bodyguards. Quite a few things about Vince were making me laugh now. I might tell him about them sometime.

Tuesday night at *TKD*, I did some proper fighting. I had to – Greg called me out to spar against him. When you spar, you're not supposed to hit or kick your partner hard. Greg is a Black Belt Fourth Dan, and I could hardly hit him at all! It was like trying to fight a shadow. A couple of times he deliberately slowed down, and I landed (well, almost landed) a side kick on him.

When we stopped, I was gasping and sweating. Greg wasn't even puffing. He nodded and said 'Good.' I felt brilliant. Bet the crafty sod had done it on purpose.

The moment I got home, Mum called, 'Ryan?' Her voice was high, twangy-sounding. My guts started heaving.

She saw the look on my face, and spoke quickly. '*Victim Support* rang, love. Tara's being moved out of Intensive Care tomorrow. She's going into a recovery ward.'

My head felt heavy. I didn't speak. 'They still don't know about the brain damage. But she's going to live, Ryan. She's going to live.'

It was too important for me to do or say anything. Too important to laugh or howl. Mum put one hand against my cheek and leaned her forehead against mine.

In my room, I sat without moving on the edge of my bed. I felt as if I was holding a cup filled with something incredibly precious. If I did anything, or even thought anything too suddenly, it might spill. Suddenly I pictured the court charge I still had to face. Now it wouldn't be . . .

Over and over through my mind went the words, 'You'll be OK now. You'll be OK now.' I wasn't sure who I was saying them to.

CHAPTER TWELVE

TARA:
The light had changed. I was moving – there were wheels under me. A car? That car. Oh shit, no . . .

RYAN:
I kept slogging away at school work on Wednesday. Didn't see Vince much. Didn't care much. Ash was around, saying as little as usual, but just being there. I was going to ask about him and that hot Mel chick, but I didn't want to hear anything about bloody Brittany. I went for a run before tea, watched some TV with Jon, went to bed early. I'm making up for the nights I didn't sleep, I suppose.

Jon spoke just as I was heading off for bed. 'You know, mate – I was a wild driver when I was a young guy. If anybody hit someone, it . . . well, feels like it should have been me, not you. Dunno if that makes any sense.'

Nah, not really. Not much sense at all. But I guess the thought did.

Twelve days after admission, the patient was transferred to Ward 11 (Recovery Ward). Spastic twitching of the legs continued. The tracheotomy tube remained in place, in case there were problems with airway blockage.

RYAN:

Ash told me at school on Thursday how Mel said people have been sending heaps of cards and flowers and things to Tara. Some Chinese guy and a woman even turned up with a big stuffed dog.

Nobody else was there when I got home. I stood staring out of the window for a bit. Then I flicked through the phone book for the number I was after, and rang the Gowers. It should have been *Victim Support*, but Mrs G had said . . .

A voice answered. 'Hi, there's nobody here just now. Leave your name and . . . ' I stood stone-still. It was a girl's voice, light and clear. Her voice; it had to be. I tried to say something, but my throat was jammed. I put the phone down.

Jon was doing overtime at work; I'd heard him and Mum talking bills at breakfast. She was doing some study for her Office Skills Course. About eight o'clock, I rang the Gowers again. My fingers went tight as the phone burred at the other end.

Mrs G answered. Her voice was tired. Yes, Tara was in a room in the Recovery Ward. They were still waiting for the sedation to wear off completely.

'Can I –' I took a breath and tried again. 'I wonder if I could see her sometime? Just to say I'm sorry.'

Silence at the other end. Finally her mother said, 'We'll have to think about that, Ryan. The doctors say she'll probably have no idea what happened, but we don't want anything that might upset her. We certainly don't want her knowing who you are. I'll get back to you.'

They didn't want their daughter knowing – I was supposed to be some sort of mongrel, was I? Yeah, I guess I was, as far as they were concerned. I looked at my watch. 8.09 pm. Almost exactly two weeks.

Insulin infusions continued. More extensive physiotherapy was also started, with a tilt table being used to exercise spinal muscles.

RYAN:

On Friday morning, Tara's father rang. I heard Mum say, 'Hello, Richard', and stopped with a chunk of toast half in my mouth. She listened, said, 'I'll get him', and passed me the phone.

Mr G sounded polite but careful. 'Tara's Mum and I have talked it over, Ryan. We're not all that thrilled with the idea, but yes, you can come and see her. Just for a few moments. The hospital says they want to stimulate her, but not tire her.'

I hesitated, then asked if I could come that afternoon. 'All right,' he said. 'But don't expect anything. We're not sure if she can hear anything. She hasn't opened her eyes yet.'

Mum didn't say much when I told her. I could tell she still didn't like the idea. At school, I told Ash and Vince, too. Vince said nothing, surprise surprise. At the end of lunchtime, as I was heading off for the Computer Room, Ash suddenly went, 'I'll come. I'll hang around in Reception.'

I said thanks, and hoped I'd have had the guts to do it for him.

TARA:

Underneath me, something moved. My back lifted up. That car – Then there was a hand stroking me, and I could smell soap or lotion. Who was . . . ? I had to find out.

On the fifteenth day after admission, there were indications that the patient was trying to open her eyes.

RYAN:

Ash and I got a bus to Central Hospital. Jon had the *Subaru* at work, and anyway, I still felt edgy about driving.

Ward 11 was one floor below I.C.U. We came through the doors into a biggish reception area, with chairs and a TV set. Half-a-dozen people were sitting around, and suddenly I saw another reason Ash had come. Two of the people were Mel and Brittany.

Dark-haired Mel smiled at us. She sure was cute. Brittany gave me the same glare she had outside Southside Plaza. She sure wasn't cute. 'What do you want?'

I wasn't taking any more bullshit from her. 'It's none of your bloody business.'

'You think –' she fired up. But I bulldozed straight over her. 'Just shut it, eh? I know you're her friend, and you hate my guts. Shit, do you think I'm not sorry? You think I wouldn't give anything if this never happened?'

It was the first time I'd said it out loud, and I could feel myself shaking. I'd held my voice low, but the other people in the reception area were watching. Brittany kept glaring.

Ash spoke suddenly. 'He's right, Brittany. This guy is gutted.'

Mel's big dark eyes watched me. Brittany began to snarl something, then stopped and looked past me. I turned, and Tara's father was coming towards us.

He gave us a tired smile. 'Didn't expect such a crowd. Probably be best if just two of you come at a time.'

Mel said, 'I'll wait.'

There was silence for a second. Brittany and I looked at each other. 'OK?' Mr Gower asked. So we headed off (me and this chick who hated me), for the room of her friend, whose life I'd maybe ruined forever . . .

CHAPTER THIRTEEN

Tests on the seventeenth day after admission showed no change in the different sizes of the patient's pupils. This, plus continued spastic twitching in her legs, caused concern that there could be damage to frontal areas of the brain.

RYAN:

I expected to be scared. I wasn't: I was bloody terrified.

We walked along the corridor, Brittany striding ahead of me. Her head was up and her neck stiff. I saw the parting in her fair hair, and remembered that other, brown-haired head swinging as it turned to face me.

The door to Tara's room was slightly open. A screen stood behind it. The curtains were closed, so everything was dim and green-coloured, like stepping into a place under the sea.

'They're trying to keep things restful and quiet.' Mr Gower pushed open the door. Ahead of me, Brittany's shoulders lifted as she took a deep breath. I did the same, and in we went.

TARA:

Voices had been talking. I couldn't tell how long ago. There was something soft in my hand. I wanted to turn my head and look at it. I wanted to turn my head and look at it!

RYAN:

Tubes and machines. Tubes everywhere. One up her nose, another in her arm. One – oh shit – leading into her throat.

In a corner of the room, screens like little TV sets glowed. Coloured lines ran or pulsed across them – red, green, blue. HEART, read the words beside the green line; BLOOD PRESSURE and OXYGEN beside the red and blue ones. I didn't have time to read the others. Beside the bed stood a tall, white stand with plastic bags of liquid hanging from it, leading to the tubes in her nose and arm.

She lay among it like an animal in a laboratory. She was on her back, head raised slightly, eyes shut. She looked skinnier than I remembered. I suppose they could only feed her liquids.

Her hair was brushed back. No – I jerked as I saw. It had been shaved off above her forehead on one side. There was a patch where something had been stuck to the skin. That whole part of her head was a mass of greeny-yellow bruising.

Above the bed, dozens of paper dolls and cards hung where she could see them if . . . if she ever saw. Someone had slipped a fluffy toy dog under her right hand where it lay outside the covers. Ash had mentioned some Chinese guy.

Beside me, Brittany breathed in little gasps. I couldn't make a sound. Tara's mother sat at the head of the bed. She was taking cream out of a jar, and stroking it gently on to the girl's neck. I felt like some pervert watching through a bedroom window, and I stared at the floor.

Mrs Gower murmured in her daughter's ear. 'Tara, love. Brittany's here again. And Ryan. You don't know Ryan, but he wants you to get better. You might . . . you might like to talk to him later.'

Nah. She wouldn't ever want to talk to a shit like me. Brittany didn't say anything, but I knew she thought the same.

TARA:

Someone was speaking. Someone I knew, saying names. I wanted to see. I was way down in the dark, but I wanted to see.

RYAN:

'Hi, Tara.' Brittany's voice wobbled. She got out a few sentences about their Summer League netball team, and someone called Ms Gilchrist, and how they all reckoned it was time Tara was back playing for them, even if she did drop passes. 'The Rockets aren't firing without you,' she managed to say, then stood there swallowing.

So she – Brittany – belonged to some team called Rockets? Maybe that's why she was always blazing off. Mrs Gower looked at me as if she was waiting for me to speak. I shook my head.

'How is she today, Mrs G?' Brittany had got her voice back to something like normal.

Tara's mother gave a nod. 'She's coming along, aren't you, love?' She stroked the still figure's cheek. Her own face was haggard; she didn't look as if she believed her words. 'It's early days yet. We're in no hurry, are we, honey?' No sound from the girl on the bed.

I remembered that magazine article about the other girl with the head injury, and how she'd taken months to . . . Then I saw something. My eyes fixed, and my throat locked tight.

Brittany was talking to Mrs Gower. 'Is there anything I can bring next time? Anything you'd like me to do?'

Tara's mother shook her head. 'Thanks, Britt. Just keep coming. Let her feel that people are here. I'm helping with the physio; moving her arms and legs. You can –'

But then my throat unlocked and I stopped them. 'Look! Look at – her eyes are open.'

After damage to the brain, the whole nervous system may be thrown into a state of trauma, which depresses brain activity. As the shock wears off, activity patterns may reappear. Anything that stimulates a recovery should be encouraged.

RYAN:

Both her eyes were open, flickering, half-closing, twitching open again. They weren't seeing anything – I knew that straightaway. For a second, they seemed to stare at me, then their lids started to sink shut again.

'Tara, love? Darling, it's me.' Mrs Gower was stooped over the bed, face almost touching her daughter's. Mr G had stepped forward and was bending over too, tense as a stretched wire. 'Tara?'

The eyelids jerked apart for a second, then closed again. 'Tara? Darling – Tara?' Mrs G's knuckles went up to her mouth. Her husband put his arms around her.

A nurse bustled into the room, plump and blonde and smiling. 'Time for Tara to have her wash. You want to help with that again, Sally?'

Mrs Gower's voice rasped. 'She opened her eyes. For about four – five seconds. She opened her eyes.'

The nurse kept smiling. 'That's good. Doctor will be pleased to hear that.' She turned to Brittany and me. 'We'll have to shoo you lot out now.' Bloody idiot – didn't she realise what had just happened!

We walked back down the corridor to reception, saying nothing. It was the longest silence I'd heard from Brittany and I was grateful for it.

TARA:
I felt my eyes strain and move. There was light and colour, all blurred and swimmy. The voices stopped. Had I made a mistake? Was I in the wrong place? Why didn't Mum or Dad tell me something?

It was all too much. The voices started again, but I couldn't be bothered. I gave up.

CHAPTER FOURTEEN

RYAN:
Ash and Mel were talking, heads together. She was smiling at him; I suddenly wished like hell some girl would smile at me. Huh – no chance of that just now. It was totally unfair, I told myself for the ten thousandth time. Other people made mistakes when they were driving and got away with it. But not me. Brittany sat down, staring at nothing. 'How is she?' Mel asked, but the other girl just shook her head.

'Let's go,' I said to Ash. I had to get outside, into the fresh air. I hesitated, then told Brittany, 'You were good.' She didn't look at me.

I thought I'd sleep that night, but I was awake a lot. About three o'clock, I sat on the edge of my bed, looking out at the garden shadows again. Something sped down the dark night sky. A meteorite. A speck of dust maybe eighty kilometres high, burning up in the Earth's atmosphere. We'd learned about them in Science. A sign of . . . something. I had no idea.

After the patient was settled in Ward 11, her parents were given reading material explaining the slow nature of recovery from head injury. They were encouraged to be realistic but hopeful, and reminded that it was still early days.

RYAN:

The weekend went fast. Time's speeded up since I knew she was going to live. Saturday morning, I slept in till ten. Must have been making up for the night. Mum and Jon yawned and drank coffee and read the paper and yawned some more.

I did a couple of hours on a Food Technology assignment. I can write well. Yeah, sounds like I'm so up myself, but it's true. Just like it was true that someone else was in hospital, with her life and education and everything going nowhere.

In the afternoon, Vince and I did some more car-polishing for his old man. Everything I said, he went, 'Yeah' or 'Right.', like some little kid scared he'd get into trouble if I told on him. Three weeks back, I knew that Vince and I would be mates forever. But that was three weeks back.

When I came home, there was a letter waiting for me. I saw the word POLICE on the envelope, and I knew. The Youth Aid Section wanted me to attend a conference where the road accident causing injury to Tara Melanie Gower would be considered. So the next stage was coming.

TARA:

I was at the bottom of a swimming pool. I could breathe, but I wanted to get up, see above the surface. People were calling to me, slow and far away. Mum. Dad. Someone from . . . school. Someone with strange English.

A couple of times I got near the surface. I started to see colours and lights. It was all blurry, and then I sank down again.

My whole body ached. People kept touching me and moving me. Some of it was nice; some just made me feel tired. Why didn't they leave me alone?

Something really scary had happened. There was a car; I know that now. Faces inside it. My mind didn't want to think about it.

By the start of the fourth week, the patient was more awake and beginning to move. However, she still did not seem to be responding to other people. Physiotherapy with the tilt table continued. The tracheotomy and naso-gastric feeding tubes remained.

RYAN:
TKD on Sunday. Greg put me through a really hard pattern of kicks and blocks. I was just finishing when I saw someone standing and watching. Ash. My stomach tightened. Then he grinned, and I relaxed again.

'Thought I'd watch the fighting machine in action,' he said, after we'd done our final stretches. 'Hey, got some good news. Mel's been up at Central again. Tara's moving and making noises.'

I stared. 'What sort of noises?'

Ash shrugged. 'Mel said they were like little grunts and things. But that's cool, eh?'

I didn't know if it was or not. Couldn't she talk? But Ash was going on. 'She's opened her eyes a few more times too, Mel says. Her parents keep telling her to nod her head if she can hear them.' He hesitated. 'She hasn't, yet.'

I did sleep well on Sunday night. So well that I spent half of Monday yawning. Most kids at school have forgotten the accident. Some of my mates ask, 'Any news?' but you can tell it's over as far as they're concerned. Like I said, people are so separate.

I rang *Victim Support* on Monday afternoon. When the phone went an hour later, it wasn't them. It was Mr Gower. Yes, Tara was moving her legs and arms, though the doctors couldn't tell how much was deliberate. She wasn't twitching, the way she'd been before. The hospital was thinking of getting her to start sitting in a wheelchair, to help strengthen her muscles.

A wheelchair. That had to be good. 'I – Can I see her again?'

Silence for a second. When Mr G answered, I could hear the tiredness. 'Yes – just for a little while, you understand. Thursday.'

TARA:

Time passed. I knew that. Sometimes things were dark and quiet. Other times there were people moving. The soft, fluffy feeling in my hand had gone – why?

I thought about it while more time went past. The place where I was grew dark again, then people and noises came back. Why didn't they give me that fluffy thing? I was getting pissed off with them. They talked at me all the time, but they never listened. So I'd make them listen. I opened my eyes. It was all bright and blurry again. Things kept coming and going. But I half-saw someone. Mum?

RYAN:

So I went to school on Tuesday. And Wednesday. And Thursday. I coached the juniors at *TKD*, and Greg said, 'Good focus, mate.' I got eighty-six per cent for my IT assignment.

The house was empty when I got home on Thursday. Mum was doing work experience for her Office Skills course. I made myself a sandwich and caught a bus to Central Hospital.

As I pushed through the double doors into Ward 11, an Asian couple came towards me, talking quietly. She had her hand on his arm. I held the door for them: the woman said, 'Thanks you', and the man smiled. I was half-a-dozen steps into the ward when I remembered Ash mentioning a Chinese guy bringing a stuffed dog for Tara. I looked back. He was standing by the doors, watching me.

The door to her room was slightly open. Someone murmured on the other side – her mother. I wanted to turn and walk away. But I sucked in some air and knocked. Mrs Gower called, 'Come in.' I stepped inside, and the girl was looking at me.

CHAPTER FIFTEEN

RYAN:
She knew I was there. Knew something was there, anyway. Her eyes moved as I came in, then they went vague. Tubes still led into her nose and throat, but a couple of the machines seemed to have gone. Her hair around the shaved patch on her head was starting to grow, and the bruises were fading. The Chinese guy's toy dog sat on a table by her bed. The paper dolls stirred in a little breeze.

Once again, I couldn't say anything. I seemed to be spending lots of time just now with my mouth hanging open. Tara's mother stroked her daughter's forehead. 'Here's Ryan, love. He came to see you before, with Brittany, remember?'

'Hi,' I managed. 'I . . . hi. How are you?' Shit, I must have sounded a total retard.

'Ryan knows Mel, too, love,' Mrs G went on. 'They've been in a couple more times,' she told me.

'Yeah. Yeah, I know.' I was staring at a photo propped against the fluffy dog. A girls' netball team: must be . . . The Missiles, was it? Nah, The Rockets. There was Mel, looking so hot. Brittany, looking like she might punch the photographer. And, yeah, her, on the end. All those chicks' legs, I thought, then felt like some pervert again.

I glanced away, and there was the unmoving outline under the bedclothes. Suddenly I felt so sorry for her that I just ached. It didn't matter a stuff whose fault it was. The only thing that did matter was helping her be like she was in that photo again.

Her eyes were closing. 'You have a rest, love,' Mrs Gower told her.

She made a noise. A little grunt, like Ash had said, but it was a human noise. The ache swept through me again.

Her mother talked quietly to me for a while: about what a nice boy Ash was; how Mel liked him (yeah, lucky Ash); about how her husband said Jon was an excellent auto-electrician.

Afterwards, I sat in one of the reception area chairs and stared at my hands. 'Are you waiting to see someone?' asked the woman at the counter, and I shook my head. No, I was waiting to see if I could make it home.

TARA:
Mum was there again. I knew how to open my eyes now, but it was hard sometimes. I felt so weak. One time Mel and Brittany were there, though I couldn't see them clearly. Britt looked wild; I must be late for practice or something. I wanted to say sorry. Then I wanted to tell her to stop being shitty so often, but it wouldn't come.

And then this guy – I'd seen him somewhere. He just stared at me; he'd done that before, through a window or something. Did I have a zit on my face? He must be Mel's boyfriend. Mel has heaps of boyfriends. I wish . . .

On Day Thirty, the patient was moved for the first time into a wheelchair. This was to encourage muscle recovery, and to promote greater interaction with people.

She was now responding to sounds, though she sometimes did not seem to know where those sounds came from. Her eye response to light or movement remained erratic. The difference in pupil size continued to cause concern.

TARA:
I was in a different place. My head was up and wobbly. I was on a bike. No, I don't ride a bike now – it's not cool at high school. Dad was there. Dad doesn't ride a bike, either. He'd look a total geek. Jeez, why do parents behave like geeks?

That guy I saw. I don't know him but I do. I try to remember, but I can't. I'm tired.

RYAN:
No word from Vince. A weekend, and I didn't hear from my best mate.

Except he wasn't my best mate any more. I'd been half-thinking it; I'd shoved it away, but while we were polishing those cars last weekend, I finally knew. Funny, really – you never think about a friend changing like that. OK, you have these bust-ups at primary school, and you tell the other kid you hate them, they're not your friend any more. But now . . .

Ah well, shit happens.

Saturday morning, I sat around a bit. Saturday afternoon, Ash rang and asked if I wanted to come and watch netball. He meant Mel's team, surprise, surprise.

I told him no. There was this girl who would be there, called Brittany. And there was this girl who wouldn't be there, called Tara, plus all the others in the team who knew why.

By Day Thirty-two, the patient's eye movements were becoming more purposeful. She was making sounds, but there was no vocalising of words, even when the tracheotomy was blocked to help her.

RYAN:

The Police Youth Aid meeting was set down for Tuesday, after school. Sunday, I went to *TKD* and worked with the juniors on their basic patterns. Then I talked to Jon while he fitted a new magneto on the *Subaru*. My old man, Mr Non-Event, never had time to talk.

I didn't go to the hospital. Too many other people go there over the weekend. But I rang the Gowers, and Mr G said Tara had been in a wheelchair yesterday and today, and seemed to be noticing things. When I hung up, I felt giddy, like when I breathed myself full of oxygen for a *TKD* fight.

Monday. Thirty-two days since it happened. Over a month.

I got a jolt at school. Vince came charging up as I was heading for Form Period, and started raving on about how he'd gone away for the weekend with his old man who was seeing about some car franchise, and the guy his old man was dealing with had these two really hot daughters . . .

I half-listened to him for a minute, then I said 'Gotta go', and walked away. I could feel him staring after me. If he tried to say anything, I was going to bloody turn around and whack him. But he just let me go. What I'd been thinking over the weekend was true, all right.

After school, I headed for the hospital. I knew the way so well by now that I recognised some of the bus drivers. I went up to Ward 11, checked with the woman at reception, walked along to Tara's room, and the bed was empty.

The same sick fear ripped through me. Her heart had stopped a second time. Or something else had gone wrong, and they'd rushed her back to Intensive Care.

A noise came from behind me. I spun around, and there she was in a wheelchair. Her father was pushing her, and he had a big grin across his face. 'Just been having a turn down the corridor. Ryan's come to see you, Tara.'

She made another of those little grunting sounds. She was watching me, brown eyes wide and unblinking. A person was behind there, all right. Again I had to look away.

She wore a nightie or a long T-shirt. A rug covered her knees, but it was rucked up on one side, and I saw one slim, smooth leg. Yeah, human bodies were so incredible. But how well would hers ever work again?

CHAPTER SIXTEEN

Midway through the fifth week, the patient's tracheotomy tube and urinary catheter were removed. She had begun to swallow more strongly, so it was decided that the naso-gastric feeding tube might also be removed in a few days. She was showing increased awareness of her surroundings since being placed in a wheelchair.

RYAN:

At school on Tuesday, I kept wondering about the Police Youth Aid meeting. Vince asked if I wanted to go down to *McD's*, but when I told him about having to see the cops, he shut up fast. I can press buttons and make him do nearly anything now. Anything except the one thing that matters.

Jon had left us the car, and Mum made me drive. We waited a few minutes in the foyer. Then a different cop appeared, a younger guy with a moustache. 'Mrs O'Carroll? I'm Terry Smith, Youth Aid Officer. You and Ryan like to come along?'

It was the same small, bare room as last time. There was new graffiti on the table: TYRON ROCKS. We sat and listened while the cop said this was just a quick meeting to explain the Family Group Conference in about a fortnight.

The police would talk first to the Child Youth and Family Service about what had happened. Someone from the CYFS would run the conference. The official charge was now Careless Use of a Motor Vehicle Causing Injury, and the aim of the conference was to let the victim (my back still crawled at the word), or her family and friends, say whatever they wanted. The offender's family and friends could speak too. Both sides would try and decide what should happen after that. 'It's important everyone has a say,' the Youth Aid guy told us. 'This is a coming together process.'

Tara's family and friends. Shit, would they let Brittany have a go at me?

'Is there anyone outside the family you'd like to bring along?' the cop asked. Mum hesitated, and said we'd get back to him. Ash? I thought. Nah, he was in the car; it wouldn't be right.

There was another thing I had to know. 'Is there still gonna be a court case?'

The cop put on a neutral expression. 'That's not for me to say, Ryan. The Family Group Conference will make a recommendation, then the police will decide.'

It was all over in fifteen minutes. I drove home with neither of us saying much. I went to *TKD* and couldn't concentrate. 'Where are you?' Greg asked.

I walked back through the spring night, realising something on the way. In the living room, Mum and Jon had just finished talking, and they had exactly the same idea. Yeah, we'd ask Greg if he could be at the Family Group Conference.

TARA:

My face and mouth felt clear. Something had been taken away. People moved me round on the bike or whatever, and I got scared. I didn't like being moved like that; I might fall, or fly through the air. I did that once; I can remember.

Mel and Brittany were here. They brought something. I'm trying to remember that, too. Some guy . . . who?

Yeah, a picture of a guy! A real hunk in a magazine, with his shirt off. They kept holding it up for me to look at and laughing. It was so embarrassing; Mum or Dad might walk in and see it. No, they have to knock before they come into my room. Mum and I had a row about that a few times. So where did I –?

I wanted to say the guy was really hot. Then I heard this weird noise from my mouth, and Britt started to get hyped up. When I looked next, they weren't there.

RYAN:

Ash told me how Brittany and Mel took this picture of some stud up to the hospital 'to show Tara what she's missing'. He said it was Brittany's idea: huh, I'm surprised she didn't get some scissors and cut off the guy's . . .

Wednesday. Thursday. The days went by like wheels rolling. Thirty-five since it happened. For the first few of them, I'd counted every hour. Each week now, she was a bit better. But how much better would she ever get, and how long would it be? I thought of that magazine article again.

By the end of the fifth week, the patient was able to focus her eyes on people. A picture of a good-looking young man seemed to hold her interest (and the interest of nursing staff!).

She appears to understand some speech. Her movements have become more purposeful, so she was given mittens to prevent her from pulling out the naso-gastric tube.

For two nights, she was restrained in her bed with straps, because she had begun struggling and trying to get out of bed. Her parents found the restraints so distressing that her mother slept on the floor in the patient's room, holding her and talking to her each time she tried to get out of bed. After another three nights, the patient was sleeping in a more relaxed manner.

Against all these promising developments must be set the neurosurgeon's warning that complete recovery is uncertain and a continuing significant disability seems possible.

TARA:

My hands felt thick and funny. I tried to look at them, but turning my head was so hard. A couple of times I got shit-scared. I was all shut in. I had to escape. Then Mum was there, stopping me and saying things. I tried to push her away, yell, 'Sod off!' at her. But then it felt better.

I was sitting up again. I could see things, but sometimes they were blurry. More time had gone. Hey, did I need to go to the loo? I must have been, without even knowing it. Did I . . . I was worried before that I might pong. There was the smell of fish and chips. Someone who talked funny. I couldn't think who.

That guy. I kept coming back to him. I've seen him before somewhere. He's important.

I was more here now. I'd been away, I didn't know where, but I wasn't going back. I was fifteen – no, sixteen years old, and I was here.

They were pushing me down a hall. I felt a bit sick. No – I was feeling a lot sick.

RYAN:

I went to the hospital after school on Friday. I didn't tell my mates. Vince wouldn't come anyway. Ash would, but he'd probably tell Mel, and she'd tell Brittany.

I pushed through the doors into Ward 11's reception area, and started down the corridor, just as the Chinese guy came out of Tara's room. There was no time to pretend I was heading somewhere else. Anyway, he'd already stopped. 'You are friend?'

I stared at the floor, then I made myself look up. 'No. I was driving the car.'

Shit, I thought as I spoke. This guy probably knows martial arts. He'll break my neck in three places.

But he just said, 'You helper now?' It might have been 'help her'; I wasn't gonna get picky about his accent. I nodded. 'I want – yeah.'

He kept watching me. He had a face that had seen things; that's the only way I can put it. After a moment, he said, 'She is number top girl', and moved off. Any other time I might have grinned, but I'd got out of the habit of grinning.

I knocked, and Mrs Gower told me to come in. She was sitting beside Tara, who was in the wheelchair again. She nodded at me. 'Here's Ryan again, love.'

The girl wore a T-shirt with '67' on it in red letters. Someone had plaited her hair into pigtails. There were thick, white gloves on her hands, those ones without fingers, like socks. With the pigtails, they made her look like some cute little kid.

Mrs G saw me gazing at the gloves. 'They're to stop her pulling the tubes out. You're getting impatient, aren't you, darling?'

The brown eyes watched me. Her mouth was slightly open. She looked puzzled, like she was trying to work something out.

'Hi,' I mumbled. 'Hi. I like the – the socks.'

She made a noise – different from last time, a sort of gargling sound. 'She understands you,' her mother smiled.

Actually, the noise sounded more like . . . She made it again. Then her head came forward, and she spewed up over her T-shirt.

CHAPTER SEVENTEEN

RYAN:

For a few seconds, there was panic. Her mother was trying to hold her and clear the . . . the stuff from her mouth, and keep her nose tube out of the way. I was trying not to puke too. I can't stand the smell.

Mrs G pushed a button above the bed. Tara kept making little gurgling, mewing sounds. Her shoulders heaved; her eyes were frightened. I was leaning forward, passing my handkerchief (I actually had a clean handkerchief!) to her mother while I held my breath. I saw the slim neck, and some sort of patch on her throat where one of the tubes had been. I'd hardly ever been this close to a girl before, but I was too scared to notice any more. What was happening?

A nurse hurried in. 'Poor Tara. Not feeling too well, love?' Yeah, you could say that, I thought. 'Sitting up and moving can do it,' she told Mrs G. 'It's like being car-sick. Plus her brain's sending confused messages about balance just now.'

I got out of it. She'd be so shamed if she knew anyone else was there. Plus, that smell! 'I'll tell her you came,' her mother said. I wandered towards the stairs feeling useless.

TARA:

I did pong! I suddenly realised it. Oh no, it was puke; I'd spewed up, and there were people. But it couldn't be a party. Mel and Britt and I had promised one another.

That guy was here again. I think he was, anyway. He stared at me. Oh, piss off, I wanted to tell him. Can't you see I –? Then I just wanted to lie down and curl up, like you do when you're sick.

But I heard. I really heard. People were saying things. 'Sitting up . . . being car-sick . . . brain.'

That's it. There was a car, and it hit me. I'm in hospital; I must be. And before . . . there were people bending over me, trying to help me. That guy – was he there? Yeah! He must have helped me after the car hit me. Cool.

Early in the sixth week, it was decided to remove the naso-gastric tube and start feeding by mouth. The patient was now able to swallow well, and occasional vomiting made the tube inconvenient and uncomfortable.

To reduce nausea, a trans-dermal patch was applied to the skin, and changed every seventy-two hours.

TARA:

Mum was there and helping a lot. Dad, too. I couldn't see them clearly, sometimes. Some people were treating me differently from others. Some were in a hurry. Some didn't talk to me. I'm gonna tell them off when I get better. I'm gonna say thanks to Mum and Dad. When I get better.

RYAN:
Saturday morning, I helped Jon sink some posts to hold up our back fence. Jeez, I never thought I'd spend part of my weekend working in a garden. Mind you, it's not easy thinking of Jon as a gardener, either. Before he and Mum got together, he and Pio had been in the Road Ragers gang, and he was still into leathers and shaved heads and stuff. Then he met Mum and realised he had to try a different technique from burn-ups and piss-ups. (He told me this when Mum wasn't there, surprise surprise.)

Another surprise. Vince rang at lunchtime to see if I felt like hitting Southside Plaza later. 'Ash is watching netball!' he went. 'Can you believe it?' Yeah, I could, knowing who was at netball. I told Vince I'd be a starter; any friend is better than none – I suppose.

We headed downtown and wandered round Southside for a bit, while Vince told me about his latest CDs, and ranked all the chicks out of ten. He was still edgy. I could tell he was wondering if I might just walk off, like that time at school. Let him sweat, I thought.

'We'll go to *Burger King*, OK?' he said after a bit. 'I'll buy – the old man paid me heaps for flossing up a couple of cars.' So we went round the corner into the food court, and there at a table were Ash and Mel. And Brittany.

As soon as Vince saw Mel, he was into his big man act. Shit, you'd think nothing had ever happened. Ash wasn't fussed; nothing much fusses Ash. And Mel didn't seem to worry.

Brittany meanwhile looked at me. 'Tara saw you and it made her chuck, eh?'

COMING BACK

I could have thrown a wobbly at her. I could have said something about feeling that way when I looked at her. Instead I just shrugged and went, 'Yeah.' I stared across at the other tables. 'She's got guts, eh? Even if she spews them up.'

I half-expected her to go ballistic at me. But she was silent. I glanced at her while Vince mouthed on to Mel and Ash. Brittany sat picking at a fingernail. There were two gold studs in each of her ears.

She looked up, saw me watching, and shot me a half-glare. 'What are you going there for?'

Tara's father had asked me that, the very first time I went. 'To see if I can help,' I told her stroppy friend now. 'And 'cos I . . . I have to know.'

'Yeah?' Brittany went. 'Well it's only because her Mum and Dad say you can. Far as I'm concerned –'

Then Mel broke in. (I guess she wanted a spell from Vince; I certainly wanted a spell from Brittany.) 'Tara's Mum told us about the Family Conference thing. She said they want to keep it small. It'll probably be just her and Mr Gower, and us.'

Brittany was in like a flash. 'Bet you're shit-scared about us coming, eh?'

I've been shit-scared for weeks, I didn't say out loud.

The trans-dermal patches allowed the patient to resume sitting in a wheelchair, provided she was moved slowly. By Day Thirty-eight, she was awake for longer periods. Her vocalisation had improved, but she still had not formed any words. Physiotherapy continued, and an exercise regime was discussed.

107

RYAN:

More days slid by. Sunday, I went to *TKD*. I was going to ask Greg about the Family Group Conference, but he was tied up with some juniors' parents.

Monday, school. Tuesday, school then *TKD*. I told Greg about the Conference, and asked if he'd maybe write or say something. He watched me so long, I thought he was going to say No. Then he nodded. 'I'd be honoured, Ryan.' Jeez, he'd be honoured?

Wednesday, and I was just leaving for school when the phone rang. It doesn't scare me now, so I just waited by the door while Mum answered. Then I heard her voice go serious. 'Of course. Yes. Yes, we'll be there.'

It couldn't. Not now, when Tara was so much better. My hand clenched on the doorknob. Mum came through and saw me. 'It's all right, love. It was Child and Family – the Conference is next Wednesday morning.' I breathed deep all the way to school. I remembered Brittany was going to be there, and I breathed even deeper.

TARA:

I was lying down again. People moved my arms and legs, and talked to me. Then more time disappeared, and I was sitting up. Was I gonna spew, like that other time? No . . . No, I wasn't. And my nose was clear now. Something else had gone.

I must be getting better. How long had I been in hospital? Could be ages, four or five days even. Now I'm coming back. Hope that guy comes back too, so I can thank him for helping.

People were moving my legs some more. Let me do it, I thought, and I tried to shift them. My right leg stirred. My left leg didn't. 'Good girl, Tara,' went a voice. I knew who it was.

She was blurry at first, then I saw her clearly. My mother, smiling down at me. Her face was skinny. What had happened to her?

I began to ask, and heard my voice make a weird noise. Yeah, that had happened before. I thought for a moment, then I swallowed, and whispered, 'Mum?'

Her whole face changed. Her eyes stared. Her hands flew up and pressed against her cheeks. Then she started crying.

CHAPTER EIGHTEEN

Near the end of the seventh week, the patient began vocalising words: 'Mum . . . Dad . . . Yes. She also understood more.

Skills and behaviour patterns were reappearing, but one concern was that the patient seemed to have difficulty reading even the large letters on the eye chart. It remains to be seen whether visual and/or comprehension abilities have been lost.

There also seems to be a weakness on her left side, including her left arm and leg.

TARA:

I wasn't wearing those gloves any more. And sometimes I felt myself swallowing things. Orange juice. A chocolate milkshake – my favourite! I didn't feel so sick when I was pushed in the wheelchair. Yeah, I knew it was a wheelchair now. One time, the moving made me scared I was going to puke again, so I thought, and I said, 'Stop!' It came out faint and weird, but they understood. I'm doing new stuff all the time now.

What do I know? There was a car, and it hit me. I can't remember where it happened, or why I was there. I keep thinking there was a shop or something, but I don't know. I don't know who the car driver was, either. What sort of shit is he? Yeah, I bet it was a he.

Another thing: I don't know what I look like now. I can't tell how my face feels. I can't tell if anything's happened to it. If I end up looking like some sort of freak because of that driver, I'll bloody rip him open.

That guy who helped me. I want to thank him. Maybe Mel and Brittany know him. Mel knows lots of guys. They all want to know her. Britt scares them!

RYAN:
I went to see her again on Friday. Mr Gower told me on the phone that she wasn't being sick now. Wonder what they did with my handkerchief?

There was nobody at reception. I hung around, then I wandered down the corridor to her room. I still got a jolt when I saw TARA GOWER on the door. I knocked, but nobody answered. I knocked again, stood there feeling stupid, said, 'Hello?' and went in. Maybe she was asleep.

She wasn't asleep. She wasn't there. The bed was empty.

Another stab of panic shot through me. Then I realised they must have taken her somewhere in the wheelchair.

The cards still hung over her bed. The Chinese guy's fluffy dog sat on a bedside table. Somebody had put a doctor's stethoscope round its neck. A sweatshirt or something lay on her pillow. Suddenly I felt like a peeping tom in a girl's bedroom. (I've never actually been in a girl's bedroom, but I guess . . .) I hurried out.

I was wandering back down the corridor when a voice called, 'Ryan?' Tara's mother was sitting in a little office-type room, talking to a couple of nurses.

'This is Ryan,' she told them. 'He comes to visit Tara.' The two nurses smiled at me. One was a nice-looking red-haired chick, though a bit old – twenty or so. But I didn't notice her that much, because I was still taking in what Mrs G had said. So she hadn't told anyone that I was the one who . . .

'Tara's off having another eye test,' she told me. 'I'll come and wait in reception with you.' She grinned at the two nurses. 'I've caught up on all the hospital gossip now, thanks.'

We sat in reception, and she told me about the physio Tara was having, and the words she was saying. (Brilliant!) 'They're talking about moving her to Watson House in a week or so. That's the Rehabilitation Unit over by Jubilee Park – it's got masses of physio equipment. They want to start her exercising as soon as she can.'

She turned her head from side to side, rubbing her neck, and I saw again how stressed she was. 'This Family Group Conference next Wednesday,' she went on. 'Richard and I aren't coming along to blame anyone, Ryan. We're just glad of the chance to talk it all out. Please tell your Mum that.' I nodded.

She looked at me, and I knew something different was coming. 'Ryan, there's one thing you have to remember. Tara doesn't know who you are. We've been showing her family photos, and she's forgotten some people. Her dad and I are worried what she'll do when she finds out about you. Please don't say

112

anything to her. We think it's maybe better if she already knows you a bit, but we don't want her being set back.'

When were people going to stop treating me like I had some disease? But I nodded again. 'You reckon . . . maybe I should stay away for a bit?'

'Till after next Wednesday, perhaps. We might talk about it then. We don't want her to feel we've been playing some sort of sneaky trick on her.'

She glanced at her watch. 'I'd better go get her. We want to find out why she's seeing some things blurry.'

I went down the stairs into the bright outside world. Seeing things blurry: did that mean she'd be . . . ? It was another bloody worry to try and take on board.

TARA:
I had a fright. Mum showed me a calendar. I couldn't read the figures properly, but I saw she was pointing to a date. November 4? No, November 14. 'Now,' she was saying. 'That . . . now.'

Something was wrong. When was I hurt? It was . . . no, I couldn't remember. But the weather was cold and raining; I remember that much. And it was dark, not like November.

I wanted to ask. I thought and I swallowed and I made my mouth move. The words whispered out. 'When . . . car?'

Mum started telling me. I couldn't understand all of it, and I saw she was getting upset. I started to feel scared, too, and I began getting wild at her. November 14? Why couldn't she make sense?

After a while, Dad was there. Mum and he sat and

smiled at me. His face is skinnier, like hers. Maybe they're on a diet.

I feel skinny, too. Good – my bum was too big, anyway.

The patient was now returning to a more normal sleeping pattern, with some daytime rest periods. Arrangements were begun to transfer her to Watson House. Further eye tests were discussed, to investigate her vision problem.

RYAN:
The weekend flew past. The back fence Jon and I had fixed fell over, so we fixed it again.

Monday came and went. Forty-six days. Three more till the Family Group Conference. But the really important thing now would be when Tara found out who I was. That and her not seeing things properly. How would I handle either of those? How would she handle it?

TARA:
Mum and Dad kept showing me photos, and talking about the people in them. I understood them part of the time, but then I'd drift off, and I couldn't remember what they'd told me. Pissed me off! Couldn't they take things more slowly? They said I was going to see someone called the Watsons. Never heard of them.

Most of the photos were of Mum and Dad and me. Plus there was Auntie Tamsin and her boyfriend. His name is . . . shit, I can't think. There were some of Mel and Britt and me at – that's right, at my sixteenth birthday, all grinning and pulling idiot faces. I looked at them, then I made myself smile. It felt so weird – my face muscles were all weak and the left side of my mouth wobbled as it turned up. But it was a smile.

I wanted to ask Mum about that guy who helped me. The one who was here. I kept getting flashes of the car, but it was all far away, like it happened to a different person. I saw the car, then I saw him. And there was something else.

CHAPTER NINETEEN

The patient could now make quite rapid 'lalalala' noises when asked. Her voice was growing stronger, and her fine-motor skills were improving. Her hearing was 95/100. Eye tests showed she was still having difficulty reading letters on the chart. This does raise concerns that her accident may have resulted in some loss of visual ability.

RYAN:
On Tuesday, I told my Form Teacher I was going to be away for part of tomorrow morning, 'cos there was a Family Group Conference I had to go to. I must have sounded like a lawyer. Or a crim.

When I got home, Mum said the Children Youth and Family Service had rung to confirm things. Some woman called Denise; she said it would be us and Greg and the Gowers, Mel and Brittany, and the Chinese guy. His name was Han Ze Minh; Mum had written it down. Tara worked at his Takeaways place; she'd been there just before it happened. I had no idea why he wanted to come.

Greg didn't say anything about it at *TKD*. He got me to take the Juniors again. I used to hate that; I wanted to be slamming away at things with the other seniors. But I didn't mind now.

TARA:

Our team was in the Summer League Netball. I was remembering heaps of things now. And our coach was a teacher. A Maths teacher, called . . . shit, how annoying! Hey, I had an assignment to do for her. Wonder if I managed to slither out of it.

I mucked the team up. They came here to tell me one time. No, it was a photo. And I didn't muck them up; it was that bloody driver. I wonder if the guy who helped me knows him.

RYAN:

I went to school for the first two lessons on Wednesday. Ash said, 'Good Luck', and for a moment, I wished I'd asked him to come. Vince was out in the courtyard, trying to chat up some new chick.

Jon and Mum picked me up, and we drove downtown to the Citizens' Advice Bureau, where the conference was being held. Vince should be here, I thought again. But he wouldn't be. I'd given up hoping he would. It should have made me feel down. Instead I felt as if something that had been dragging at me had suddenly fallen away.

I'd had this stupid worry in case they'd stuck a policeman outside the door or something so when I got out of the car and saw a guy in a Security Guard uniform waiting on the steps, I thought, Aw, no! Then I saw it was Greg. I knew that was his job, but I was just so used to him in his *TKD* gear.

The Chinese guy – Ze Minh – was just arriving, too. He wore a tie and a blue jacket. He came over and shook hands with Mum and Jon and Greg. 'I am not a rival,' he said.

117

Tara's parents were next, looking tired. Greg introduced himself to them, and I realised I should have done it. The Youth Aid cop from last week arrived – in an ordinary car (phew!). I heard footsteps behind me, and there were Mel and Brittany – Mel with her big eyes; Brittany with her big mouth. Mum looked like she was waiting for me to introduce them. No way. I remembered how in The History of World War II, we'd read about the Battle of Britain. Now I was facing the Battle of Brittany.

A tall woman with red hair swept into the car park, hurried over to us, and said, 'Hello, I'm Denise Metcalf. Sorry I'm late; my five-year-old's got measles.'

She waved hello to the woman in the Citizens' Advice Bureau office, and led us through into a room with a circle of chairs. 'It's really good of you all to be here.' She smiled at me like I was doing her some favour. 'I hope you'll all find this a worthwhile conference.'

She told us what would happen. The family of the victim (my back crawled again) were welcome to say anything they liked – how they felt about what had happened; what it had done to them; what should happen now. Any friends of the victim – Denise nodded to Ze Minh, who was sitting straight in his chair, polished black shoes together – could speak also. Then the family and friends of the offender (another word I had to face) were welcome to speak as well. A nod this time to Greg.

After that, the offender and his family could discuss among themselves what they thought should be done, and see if the victim's family agreed. I listened, and hoped I wouldn't screw it up.

Tara's mother and father didn't take long. They said their main feeling was relief that Tara was starting to recover – and worry while they waited to see how much better she'd get. They wished she could have been here, and they wanted me to remember what a huge chunk had been taken out of her life.

They didn't feel any anger now; they knew I was sorry. (Mr Gower suddenly looked at me then, and went 'I was angry, son. More angry than I knew I could be.' Mrs G squeezed his hand.) They just wanted me to be aware that the effects on Tara could go on forever, and to try and make sure I never caused anything like it again.

Next came Mel and Brittany. Mel just said, 'We want Tara to get better. That's all that matters.' It was short and sensible. Somehow, though, I'd expected a bit more.

Then Brittany. I'd no idea what she'd say, but I wasn't going to let her think she was getting at me. She started by saying that Mel was right. Then she looked at me. 'You told us you were sorry. I don't know if you are. Maybe you're just sorry for yourself.' (I twitched at that, but I made myself sit still.) 'Anyway, you make sure you do everything you can to help Tara. Then I might start to believe you. And you make sure you never hurt anyone else like you hurt my best friend.'

Her voice went wobbly on the last words. Aw shit, I thought. Don't start howling. She shut up then, and Mel passed her a tissue. The CYFS woman – Denise – had a big box of them; I guess tissues get used a lot at Family Group Conferences.

119

Denise waited a second, looked at the Chinese guy, and asked, 'Mr Han? Would you like to say something?'

He spoke slowly, quietly. You could tell he was thinking out each word. He gazed at me, and I made myself look back. 'Tara is valued girl. Valued by all. We lose her help, but this is not important. She is important. Everyone must work to help her be better. You are good for doing this.' He paused, dipped his head slightly at me, and said, 'The real man is one who says sorry.'

It sounded funny. It wasn't. We were all so quiet, you could hear someone tapping on a computer down the hall. Denise said, 'Thank you, Mr Han. Now – Mrs O'Carroll, Jon. Would you like to comment?'

Mum said I was a really good kid, I'd never been in trouble before. The Youth Aid cop nodded. She knew how sorry I was, and that I wanted to help Tara any way I could. (Stick that up your . . . nose, Brittany.) She stopped for a moment, then said, 'I just want to thank Richard and Sally for their forgiveness. If anything – anything like this ever happened to my child, I hope I could be as brave and kind as they've been.' She choked up then. Jon put an arm around her. Mrs G, who was sitting on her other side, looked like she might cry too.

Jon said he was glad to be my stepfather. He mentioned how I'd paid the Traffic Infringement fine out of my own money, and I could tell the cop and the CYFS woman were pleased with that.

Then Greg. He spoke quietly and carefully, too. 'Ryan's Mum is right. He's a good kid. I believe he'll grow into a good man. At *Tae Kwan Do*, he's thoughtful and considerate. He helps people. I know he'll face up to anything he has to do.' Again there was silence at the end.

I already knew what I wanted to say. 'I'm really sorry. I'd do anything if this had never happened. It was – it was my fault. And I'll do anything else that helps Tara get better again.' I looked straight at Brittany while I said this and she stared back. 'And I appreciate how you've all treated me.'

Denise waited for a moment, then thanked us again. 'Mrs O'Carroll,' she said. 'There's an office where you and Jon and Ryan – and Greg?' She looked at my *TKD* instructor, who nodded his head 'you three can go and talk over what you think should happen next. In the meantime, I'm sure we can find some coffee or tea for everyone.'

In the office, I dropped into a chair. I felt like I'd been through one of Greg's training sessions. Mum hugged me and Jon. 'You were wonderful. Both of you.'

We talked easily, gently. We'd already decided some things – I'd offer to do a Defensive Driving Course; I'd give up my licence for as long as the Gowers wanted me to. I'd write a letter to them and Tara, saying how sorry I was. I'd keep helping the juniors at *TKD*.

After a bit, we went quiet. Something was stirring in my mind. 'Be good if there's anything else you can do for Tara herself,' Mum said.

Then I knew. I told them. Jon nodded. 'Good, mate.' Mum hugged me again.

So we went back into the other room, where the Gowers stood with Denise and Mel and Brittany, and

Greg was talking to Ze Minh. Everyone listened as we spoke. Brittany gave a sniff, but said nothing. Mr and Mrs Gower looked at each other, murmured for a minute, then nodded. Yes, if Watson House agreed, I'd work with Tara on her physio and her recovery exercises as much as I could.

At the end of the seventh week, the patient's face still sometimes looked blank and expressionless. However, she could close her eyes when asked, and her facial movements were well controlled. The left side of her body remained weak.

It was decided that on Friday, the patient would be transferred to Watson House, where Ryan O'Carroll may assist with her rehabilitation.

TARA:
I remembered two more names!

The coach of our Summer League team was Ms Gilchrist. I knew I had the name somewhere; I sort of posted a message off to my brain to find it, and after a long while, the answer came back.

And I worked in the Takeaways for Jimmy. How could I have forgotten Jimmy?? And Dolly. That's three names – awesome!

It was so funny the way I remembered Jimmy. The meals were being brought through the ward on a trolley. I smelt fish, and suddenly I knew. Jimmy's been here – to the hospital. I remembered that, too.

I didn't want to eat the fish. My stomach feels like it's shrunk. It hurts when I try to swallow much. I can handle drinks, and stuff like milkshakes, but there was

this really scary time today . . . yesterday? I'm not sure
. . . when they tried me on some soup with bits of
vegetable in it.

Mum was feeding it to me. I can't get my hands to
hold things properly yet. I managed the first couple of
spoonfuls, but then a piece of potato or something
half-stuck, and I choked and coughed till it went
down. Suddenly I knew I couldn't swallow any more.
Mum was poking the next spoonful at me, and I
started trying to pull my head away, and got panicky
because I couldn't. The soup spilled down my T-shirt,
and I was yelling at Mum and the nurse to stop. Trying
to yell, anyway; I could hear these rasping noises
coming out of my mouth. Shit! Shit! Shit! Just when I
thought I was doing really well.

Things quietened down, and Mum sat talking to
me. I wouldn't listen for a bit; I was still annoyed with
her about the soup. Then I started paying attention,
and I understood most of it. Watson House isn't
people; it's a place they're moving me to for physio
and stuff. Why do I have to go somewhere else? I like
the hospital.

Then I heard Mum say a fourth name. Ryan. The
guy who came to see me. The guy who helped – but
Mum was saying that he's from Watson House or
something, and he's going to help me while I'm there.

But I thought he was . . . Oh, I dunno. I must have got
it all wrong. Just when I think I remember something,
it's gone again. I wish the doctors or someone would
talk to me about it. I wish somebody would tell me
what I look like. The times I think about that, I get too
scared to ask.

CHAPTER TWENTY

*Rehabilitation now focused on mobility and balance.
Exercises to encourage viewing and listening should also
continue, especially as the nature of the patient's visual loss
became clearer. She should move towards being able to dress,
toilet and feed herself. Another major task would be learning
to walk again.*

RYAN:
The Gowers didn't want me to give up my driving
licence. Not while I was going to Watson House to help
Tara, anyway. Mrs G rang on Friday to say so, and to
thank me for the letter of apology I'd written to them.
(I did it as soon as I got home on Wednesday). They
agreed with my doing a Defensive Driving Course.

I don't know if there'll be a court case. I was so glad
to get through the Family Conference, I'd almost
forgotten about it. The cops will decide. Jeez, when's it
all going to be over?

TARA:
They've moved me to that place. Watson House. They
took me there this morning – see, I even knew what
time of day it was – in an ambulance.

Before we went, Mum was doing my hair in plaits. I'd managed to give it about four brushes before my arm got wobbly and she took over. Then . . . Then I took a breath. I did my thinking-and-swallowing act, and asked, 'Mirror?'

Mum wasn't too keen, but she got one. 'Remember you've been sick for a long time, Tara, love. You're much better now.'

She had to help me hold it. I couldn't focus for a moment, and I didn't realise I was seeing myself. I thought it was a photo – a photo of me looking gobsmacked. My face was sort of blank and shocked.

I heard Mum say, 'You look better every day, Tara. It'll all come right; your face is starting to fill out again.'

I kept staring. Actually, apart from the blank look, I wasn't too bad. I didn't mind my face being skinny. I looked quite . . . interesting.

They wheeled me down the corridor and into the lift. A whole lot of nurses came to say goodbye. I felt a bit shamed, 'cos I hardly recognised some of them. I suppose they'd looked after me while I was out of it.

Down at the front entrance, I breathed fresh air for the first time in . . . hell, in weeks. They'd given me a fresh skin patch so I didn't throw up in the ambulance, and they'd put dark shades on me, in case the light outside hurt my eyes. I must have looked like a cool movie star. A cool, horror movie star.

I couldn't really see out of the ambulance windows, but there were colours and noises and all the stuff you don't notice when you see it every day. It was like coming out of the movies; everything was bright and noisy and alive.

After about ten minutes, the ambulance turned into a drive. My eyes felt sore and blurry behind the shades, but I saw a big old house with curved windows. There were lawns and trees – one tree had a basketball hoop on a branch! The ambulance people wheeled me out, and up a ramp past flowerbeds and into a room like a real bedroom. 'Welcome to Tara Towers,' a nurse said.

I couldn't say anything. Someone – Mum and Dad it must have been – had filled my room with all my stuffed toys from home. Dogs, bears, monkeys, lions, even the little stupid ones people had given me as jokes. They covered the shelves and the mantelpiece and the chairs. The stuffed dog Jimmy and Dolly gave me (I knew that now, too) stood on my pillow. For a few seconds, I just stared. Then I felt something funny on my face behind the dark shades, and I knew I was howling.

RYAN:
They shifted her to Watson House on Friday. On Sunday afternoon, I drove across to see her and meet the people there. Ash said he and Mel were going, too; Mel lives near. Brittany wasn't going, because she looks after her Nana some Sundays. Poor Nana.

I parked the *Subaru* carefully – I did almost everything carefully now – and found the room. Ash and Mel were already there, and Mel gave me a smile. Man, she was such a hot chick! Those eyes: it wasn't usually girls' eyes I checked out, but hers were this amazing deep blue. Yet the funny thing was, Tara looked more interesting in some ways. Maybe because she was in bed. No, shit, I didn't mean it that way. She looked at me, and when Mel said, 'Hi, Ryan', her face changed. I thought, Jeez, someone's told her! But she didn't say anything.

Mel talked about their netball game yesterday, and how the Rockets had won for a change. Ash sat quietly as usual. Tara made noises and words. I heard 'Cool . . . Britt . . . Yeah. She looked heaps better than when I'd seen her . . . ten days ago? I felt so relieved just watching her. For a second I wanted to blurt out who I was, get the whole load off me.

I got a grip and stared around. The room was full of stuffed toys; weird, the way chicks like those. One had a vest labelled KUNG FU HAMSTER. Seriously weird.

Then I saw she'd turned her head and was looking at me. Her hair had grown so that I could hardly see the shaved patch now. She swallowed and said, 'Eye'.

Her voice came out sort of thin and whispery. I thought – What? Then I realised she'd said 'Hi'.

'Hi,' I gabbled. 'Hi. I – I'm gonna help you with physio and stuff.'

She looked puzzled. Anyone would, hearing me rave on like that. Ash and Mel were staring at me, too.

Someone knocked on the door, and a woman in a sort of nurse's tunic stuck her head in. 'Ryan? If you'd like to come along, I'll show you the Physio Room.'

I got out of Tara's room like a shot. I followed the nurse to a room set up like a small gym, with parallel bars, and mats on the floor, and benches and stuff. 'Safety is the first thing,' she told me. Her name tag read BROOKE. 'Tara must be supported at all times till she gets stronger. We'll show you what to do for each exercise, and then see if you feel all right about taking over. One of us will be with you all the time. OK?'

Yeah, OK, I told Brooke. Anything that helped Tara would be fine with me. When she found out who I was, then I'd start worrying about whether I'd be OK.

TARA:
Maybe it was being in a new place, but I was awake a lot more. They expected me to be, so I was!

Dad came in after work on the fourth day I was here. Or maybe the fifth. Anyway, I was up and dressed for the first time. (I'd managed to get my arms through the T-shirt; I still can't get my knickers on by myself, which is really frustrating – and really embarrassing.) I was sitting in the wheelchair with my shades on, and when he walked in, I was able to lift my right hand up and give him a 'Hi' wave. His face split into this ginormous grin, and he gave me a kiss. He needed a shave.

I've swallowed some spaghetti. I helped hold the dish.

I'm getting better and better, though I still can't remember a lot of things. I'm looking forward to the physio exercises. And to Ryan.

RYAN:
On Tuesday, I drove across in the late spring evening (Jeez, it'll be holidays in a few weeks) instead of going to *TKD*. The first exercise session; I felt really nervous. Ash had told me to say hi. Vince hadn't said anything. If he ever did, I'd ask him when he was going to come along and tell Tara who he was. Then I remembered she still didn't know who I was.

I got out of the *Subaru*, realised I was wearing my

black-and-silver jacket from that night, and left it in the car. The nurse Brooke took me to Tara's room. She was in the wheelchair. Her hair was done up in bunches, and her face had a bit more expression in it. There was a little puckered scar on her throat where one of the tubes had been. I went, 'Hi', and she sort of went, 'Hi' back. I couldn't really think of anything to say to her – I'm pretty useless at talking to girls – so I started wheeling her slowly along the corridor to the physio room.

I was watching the back of her head, and the smooth curve of her neck. Suddenly, this huge feeling of relief that she was really getting better rushed through me. I heard myself suck in a deep breath, and for a second, I nearly reached out and touched her hair. But I didn't; I wheeled her on.

TARA:

I wanted to say 'Hi, Ryan' when he came in, but the 'Ryan' was too hard. He looked nervous; maybe he hadn't been a nurse for long.

Then I got it. He wasn't a nurse. He was a helper, a volunteer or maybe someone doing work experience. I must have heard someone calling him my helper. He had nothing to do with a car at all. Dunno why I'd thought that.

I could feel him looking at me as he pushed me along the corridor. Just as well they'd washed my hair that morning. One time I thought he was going to say something, but he didn't. He wheeled me into the Physio Room. I'd already seen it; Brooke had taken me for a Tiki Tour the day I'd arrived. She was waiting for us.

He talked to her, then they both came over to my chair. I could see he was still nervous. 'We're just going to help you stand,' Brooke said.

He and Brooke both put an arm around my waist, took my elbows, and eased me up on to my feet. He was quite strong.

And then I started learning how to walk again.

CHAPTER TWENTY-ONE

RYAN:

She stood between the parallel bars, holding one with each hand. I could hear her breathing. Brooke was in front of her; I was right behind. 'Don't worry, we'll hold you,' Brooke said. 'Support her, please, Ryan.'

I put my hands on her hips, gripping a loop of her shorts on each side. Hell, I half-expected her to swing round and whack me. I could feel her hip bones and the warmth of her back. Her legs were right in front of me. Yeah, nice legs, though they kept trembling.

Brooke smiled at her. 'Just think about the first step.'

Tara's hands gripped the bars. Her whole body was shaking now. 'I – can't.'

'It's like speaking,' Brooke told her. 'Think first, then do it.'

A pause. The right foot lifted slightly, hung for a second, then slithered forward.

'Brilliant!' Brooke clapped, and I felt like doing the same. 'Now the left leg. I know this side is harder, but you won't fall.'

Another pause. The left leg came up, quivering. Then Tara's left hand slipped off the bar, and she crumpled sideways.

Thank God for *TKD*. I moved before I'd even thought about it, and grabbed her against me. Her hair brushed my face. She smelt clean.

'Try again,' Brooke said. Tara held the bars once more. Her left leg rose, wobbled while I braced to grab her again, then jerked forward.

'Great!' I heard myself go. We helped her back into her wheelchair, and she smiled at me. A real smile, that made her whole face move. I stood grinning back at her like an idiot.

After she'd rested for a few minutes, she tried again. This time it was easier: four shuffling steps with each foot. Her breath caught and rasped each time she moved her left leg.

By the time she'd finished, she was exhausted. 'I want – more!' she demanded, but Brooke shook her head. 'Enough for now, Wonder Woman. We'll try again in the morning. Next time Ryan comes, you can show him your sprinting technique.'

We wheeled her back to her room. Brooke sent me off to find Tara a juice while she helped her into bed. I had to go hunting for a bendy straw, 'cos she has trouble drinking from a glass. When I got back, Brooke had vanished, and Tara was asleep.

She lay half on her side, one hand next to her face on the pillow. Her hair had come loose and lay across her cheek. I stood there gawping at her; I'd never seen a girl sleeping before. After a bit, I put the juice down on her bedside table. I went out, and drove home as if the world was made of glass.

By the start of the third month, the patient was able to swallow lumpier foods, though chewing still caused difficulty. She was able to dress herself while sitting. Physio continued, with exercises to strengthen her left side. She could now almost stand up by herself.

TARA:

I woke up feeling sore. My back ached and my thighs felt wobbly. Then I remembered. I'd walked. I'd really walked!

I lay there, picturing my leg lifting up and my feet pushing forward. A different nurse came in, and I had to tell her. 'I walked.'

She laughed. 'Brooke said. And you're going to do more today.'

I did. Twice – morning and afternoon. By the time we finished, I could walk all the way along between the parallel bars, turn around (if they helped me), and walk back. Shuffle back, anyway. At the end of both sessions I was starting to feel sick again – Brooke said it was all part of getting my balance back – but otherwise it was brilliant.

Then, suddenly, I had this flashback to some netball practice where I'd jumped high in the air to catch a pass, and today didn't seem so brilliant after all. I try not to think about it, but I get this terrible feeling that I'll have to spend the rest of my life creeping about while other people can do anything they want. Jeez, when I meet that driver, I'll gut him!

Brooke got me to do other things. Picking up plastic boxes like kids' toys and stacking them inside one another; rolling pastry on a table with a rolling pin.

My left hand and arm kept skidding around suddenly, but, after a while, they started to get the hang of it.

I wondered when Ryan was coming next. When I part-fell that first time I tried to walk, and he grabbed me, it was scary at first. Then when he had hold of me, it felt . . . well, not scary.

RYAN:

Wednesday, I got seventy-two per cent for an IT programme I'd had to write. Not bad, but not as good as I've been getting. I've had other things on my mind.

Thursday, I drove to Watson House after school. Jon gets a lift with Pio when I need the car. Pio says will we please borrow his heap again, so it comes back clean like last time.

Near the House, I saw Ash with Mel. And – oh joy – Brittany. I pulled over. 'Can't give you a lift, sorry,' I said. At the same time, Ash went, 'Jeez, you better not give us a lift, mate.' He and Mel both laughed – Mel's got this little dimple in one cheek. Even Brittany half-smiled. Then she said, 'You'd better pull your finger out. They're probably waiting for you.'

They came and watched while Brooke and I worked with Tara in the Physio Room. I got her to do some *TKD* muscle-stretching exercises, lying on her back and drawing one leg up, then the other; lifting your arms up from your sides and pushing at the sky; raising your bum off the ground. She managed nearly all of them. Her left leg and arm still shook, but she was stronger than just two days ago. She said a few things. 'Move it like this . . . I can't hold.' Her talking is better, too.

Mel talked to Ash. Brittany sat watching me and Tara. I knew that if I made a mistake, she'd drop me in it. So I didn't.

One time, I glanced up at her and the others, and when I looked back at Tara, she was watching me. She gave me a smile, then looked away.

I felt like some sort of rat. Sooner or later, she'd find out who I really was, and what I'd done to her. There wouldn't be any smiles then.

The patient's speech, movement, and fine motor skills continued to improve. Finger-to-nose touching and other close-vision tasks appeared easier. Another appointment was made to examine her blurred vision. There was far more expression in her face. It was stressed that care must be taken to avoid shocks which might set back her recovery.

TARA:
Every day, I was better and stronger. I'd wait till I could say heaps of sentences, then I'd ask about the car driver. Where was he hiding?

There was still lots I couldn't remember: names of teachers; Jimmy and Dolly's shop; Auntie Tamsin's boyfriend – again! Jimmy and Dolly came to see me Friday (I could keep track of the days now). They brought me this little poem written in Chinese to hang on the wall. 'Grow like flower; stand like tree,' Dolly told me. Must have sounded funny, her and me both talking in our sort-of-sentences.

On Friday, Brooke and Mum helped me stand in front of this big, full-length mirror, and watch myself while I walked a couple of steps, then stood and wobbled on the spot. It felt so weird – this person creeping and shaking was the same one who'd been playing netball (yeah, yeah – and dropping passes) just a few months back. I promised myself harder that I'd be playing next season.

Mel and Britt dropped in on Saturday morning. Only a few games left in the Summer League. They talked about maybe taking me to see the last one. Sweet. The school term was nearly over, too. Oh, hell – I didn't have the chance to enjoy missing schoolwork!

Ryan came this afternoon. He still looked nervous when he came in, like I might blast him about the exercises or something. I was sitting on the edge of the bed. He went to move the wheelchair close, but I said 'Leave it'. I leaned forward, pushed with both hands, and stood up. Then I walked – wobbled anyway – four steps across to the chair without holding on to anything. 'Brilliant!' he said. There was this expression on his face like he'd just been let off something.

On the way to the physio room, he talked about *TKD*, and how Ash is in a couple of his classes. Sometimes he sounds like he's going to say more, then he stops.

This morning, I woke up really early, and I just lay looking out of the window of my room. The lawn outside was all glittering and glowing in the first sunlight. A blackbird went running across it, then stopped with its head on one side and seemed to stare straight at me. Life is so awesome, I thought suddenly. For a few minutes I forgot the way some stupid sod had messed up my life, and I just wanted to feel that good for ever.

CHAPTER TWENTY-TWO

RYAN:

I was planning to drive over and see Ash on Saturday
night, but Jon needed the car. I got a bit pissed off. 'You
didn't tell me –'

Jon interrupted. 'Yeah, well your Mum and I have
got a life too, mate.'

We eyeballed each other. It was the first real aggro
between us since . . . 'Sorry,' I said. Jon relaxed at the
same moment and grinned. 'No worries. Hey, you're
gettin' back to being a regular teenager, eh?'

Mum came in then. 'What are you two sniggering
about?'

'Nothin'.' Jon winked at me. 'Just boys' talk.' Mum
rolled her eyes.

I wouldn't have needed the car, anyway. Ash's
mother said he was round at Mel's (don't blame him).
I wondered if Brittany was there, too. Actually, what
did Brittany do on Saturday nights? Stayed home and
sharpened her fangs, probably.

I half thought about ringing Vince. Like I said, any
friend – but he and his old man would probably be
away. His old man has women all over the place.

I felt down. I've sort of dropped out, so far as most

of my mates are concerned. I did some study – on a Saturday night! – for the exams we've got coming up. Tomorrow looks pretty flat, too. I'm not going to see Tara; her mother says heaps of visitors come on Sunday, and Tara gets tired. Suppose she had a social life too, till I messed it up.

I kept remembering the smile she gave me on Wednesday. Like I said about Ash and Mel, I always hoped a girl would smile at me. But now I half-wish it had never happened.

TARA:
Physio twice every day. I can get from bed to my wheelchair easily now, though my left leg still wobbles. But I had a shock yesterday when I tried to write a note to Auntie Tamsin and . . . Jarrod? (No – Jacob! Yay!) My writing jerked and jumped all over the place. The page looked like I'd written it on a trampoline.

A couple of little kids who've been in Watson House long-term wheeled themselves in today to see all my stuffed toys. One fell off her father's farm bike and broke her back. One has cerebral palsy and wears a crash helmet all the time, 'cos he can't stop his head banging against things. I howled after they'd been.

Sunday lunchtime, I ate some jelly – by myself. I took it slowly, and didn't drop a single spoonful. I even tried holding the spoon in my left hand. It shook quite a lot, and a couple of times I thought I was going to stick the jelly in my ear, but I managed.

I wanted to be back at school! I missed my friends and the netball team, and I've started worrying about falling behind in my subjects. I really want to do Art Design next year. If the accident has fouled me up big-time . . . Most times I don't think about it, but today I sat gripping the arms of my wheelchair, with my right hand, mostly, and I felt so bloody wild, I shook them and shook them.

'What's this?' asked Brooke, who'd come in without my noticing. 'You trying to get lift-off?'

Mum was here all Sunday morning; Dad came for part of the afternoon; so did Mel and Britt. Wonder when I'll be able to go down to Southside Plaza with them – hit the shops and check on any hot guys. I told them about Ryan coming, but they didn't say much. I wondered if Mel fancies him. Mel's always dumping her boyfriends. Pity if she dumps Josh – no, it's Ash. Actually, I think Britt fancies him. Complicated, eh?

They were talking about taking me to watch the last netball game at the end of next week. We were talking about it; I can say heaps now, though my voice still packs up sometimes. I said, 'Hope I can see it. Things get blurry a lot.'

Mel started, 'It'll get bet –', but Britt interrupted. 'Reckon you need glasses?'

I blinked. I stared. Shit, I realised – that's why things looked blurry; that's why I missed passes at netball. There wasn't any brain damage after all! I could have hugged Britt. Instead I said, 'Me wear glasses? No way!'

RYAN:

On Sunday, Greg really put me through it at *TKD*. I spent the first part coaching the Juniors; then I did fifteen minutes' solid punch-bag work: lunge punches and blocks; side kicks that made me think my legs were going to fall off; axe kicks that made me know they had. He's never said anything about the Family Group Conference. I didn't expect him to – when you do *TKD*, you focus on nothing else. But I felt he was reminding me.

Nearly ten weeks since the accident, and sometimes I still think I'll never feel safe again. Because about five minutes before we finished, someone came into the hall. I glanced across, and my heart lurched. It was the Chinese guy – Ze Minh. Straightaway, I knew something had happened with Tara.

But he just sat down against the wall and watched. He was talking to Greg when I left; he nodded at me and said, 'Good day, Lion'. After a weird couple of seconds, I realised he was saying my name. I grinned half the way home – out of relief, mainly.

We're going away at the start of the holidays. Jon's mate Pio's uncle (got it?) has a place by the sea we can have for a week. Jon and Mum are really up for it. Dunno how I feel; it'll mess up seeing Tara. Jeez, what am I saying?

The patient was now walking up to ten metres with a frame. The ophthalmologist confirmed she had slight myopia, and should begin wearing glasses – or contact lenses when her eyes can make fine movements. It is pleasing that concerns about her vision having been affected by the accident are now over.

Her neurosurgeon agreed that the outlook was increasingly favourable, though her short-term memory loss could mean problems with work, school, reading, etc.

The patient could now talk almost normally, though her voice still sounded rather expressionless. She may be able to spend some time at home over Christmas.

TARA:

So I'm gonna get contact lenses some time – and maybe geeky glasses first! Britt should be a doctor! I won't have any excuse if I drop passes from now on. On Sunday afternoon before tea, I sat out on the side verandah, and looked at the basketball hoop on that (blurry) tree. I'll throw a ball through that before I leave Watson House. I've made my mind up.

I still can't do some things. If I stand with my eyes shut, I start to lose my balance. 'Hell,' I said to Brooke, 'I thought it was only guys who are unbalanced!' But though I make jokes about it, I'm really scared of falling. What'll happen if I hit my head again? Jeez, I could end up dribbling and wearing nappies for the rest of my life.

Brooke moved the big mirror so I could watch myself walking – staggering – along, holding on to a rail above my head, looking like something that's just come down out of the trees. A couple of mornings, she even played cards with me. I had to shuffle and deal and remember which cards I put down. I beat her once! (I cheated.)

I'm going home for two days at Christmas. Awesome! I told Mel and Britt when they came on Sunday. Ash wasn't there – wonder why.

'When's Ryan coming next?' Mel wanted to know. Yeah, she fancies him, all right. Shit, I'm not jealous, am I? Britt started to say something, then she stopped. Britt's always hard on guys.

RYAN:

Monday and Tuesday, we had some of our final school exams. I'm gonna do OK: I know that sounds up myself, but I've worked really hard. I want to do Media Studies next year; like I say, I'm getting quite good at writing.

On Tuesday night at *TKD*, we had a new instructor for part of the time: Ze Minh. Turns out he was a *Tai Chi* teacher back in China. That's the martial art where you practise moving really slowly, and focus on holding your body in exactly the right position. Sounds simple, but it's not. My back and shoulder muscles all ached afterwards.

I walked home feeling so . . . so awake. It's the only way I can describe it. I never ever want anything like the accident to happen again, but I've learned things.

Another exam on Wednesday. Before tea, I drove across to Watson House. Tara was waiting in her wheelchair, wearing shorts and a T-shirt with ROCKETS on it. I wheeled her along to the Physio Room, while she told me how she's getting contact lenses some time, and how she's going home over Christmas. Her voice sounded sort of flat some of the time, but you could tell she was really excited.

Brooke wanted us to practise throwing and catching a soft plastic ball, so Tara could work on her hand-eye co-ordination and balance. 'Don't overdo it,' she said. Tara stood with her back to the wall. I threw gentle lobs to her, and she caught about half of them. Her own throws were like little kids' ones, and I could see she was annoyed that she couldn't do them harder. I made a big act of swooping and bending to catch them. I think the *Tai Chi* helped!

After about five minutes, her legs got tired and she sat on a chair while we carried on throwing. I liked watching her concentrate as she caught and threw. She kept biting her bottom lip; it was a nice soft lip.

Another nurse stuck her head through the doorway. 'Phone, Brooke.' Tara's nurse hesitated, said, 'Keep an eye on her, Ryan', and hurried out.

Tara sent me back a couple of throws. Then I tossed her a harder one. She caught it and grinned. She tossed it back somewhere near me, and I made another big deal out of catching it. I lobbed the ball back. It bounced off her hands; she grabbed sideways for it, lurched, and fell from the chair.

For a second, it was the accident all over again. Time stopped. The brown eyes stretched wide. Then she toppled towards the floor. She was going to smack her head on the floor. She was going to be wrecked.

Somehow I got to her. I flew across the space between us and grabbed her. Her hips thudded on to the floor, but I held her head and shoulders clear.

We crouched there. She stared up at me, and I knew my own mouth and eyes were wide with shock. Then an expression I'd never seen before grew across her face, and I understood what had happened.

TARA:

It was cool sitting in the chair tossing the ball between us. It gave me a chance to keep looking at him. He's quite skinny, but he's got nice hands. He looks like he's thinking a lot of the time. I liked the way he was giving me easy throws without making it obvious.

My arms and shoulders were starting to feel shaky,

but I didn't want to stop. I sent him a useless throw; he caught it and lobbed it back. I reached for it, but I stuffed it up, like at netball, and it bounced off my hands. I twisted after it, and next minute, I was falling.

Total fear ripped through me. My head – then Ryan dived; I put one hand partway down and slowed myself, and he got his arms around me. His face was just above mine. I saw his eyes, and the fear in them. Time split apart, a picture from the past came spinning up, and I knew. He was the driver.

CHAPTER TWENTY-THREE

RYAN:

Her voice wasn't flat any longer. 'You were driving! You hit me!'

It had finally come, and I couldn't say anything. I reached out to help her back on to her chair. She shoved my hand away and hauled herself up. She sat there panting and shaking. Her eyes burned at me.

'I thought you'd come to help me. You greasy bastard! I thought you wanted –' Her voice stuck and her mouth twisted.

'I do. I'm sorry.' Shit, how feeble.

'Piss off! Go on – get out!' She was staring at the floor now. I felt scared suddenly: what if she worked herself into a fit or something? I made myself speak again. 'I'm sorry. I wasn't trying to hide it. Your Mum and Dad – they knew.'

Her head jerked up. The scar on her throat pulsed as she swallowed. Her eyes drilled holes in me. She looked awesome.

'Piss off! You lying shit!' Her left arm jerked up and I thought she was going to thump me. Instead, she started hugging herself. That made me more scared.

'I'll get Brooke,' I mumbled. I stepped out into the

hall, and Tara's nurse was coming towards me. 'How's it go –?' she began. She saw my face and stopped.

'Tara's not too good,' I managed to say. Brooke shot me a glance and hurried past.

Out in the car park, I sat in the *Subaru*, like I'd done those other times. It had finally happened, and it wasn't as bad as I'd expected. It was worse.

TARA:

I couldn't believe it. The lying shit! Greasing his way in with Mum and Dad. Why hadn't they told me? I'd murder them. And I'd thought he was quite –

Brooke bustled in. 'You all right?'

'He was the driver!' I heard my voice hiss and croak. 'He bloody put me here!'

Brooke nodded. 'I know.'

I glared at her. They'd all been lying to me. 'What's he coming here for?'

'You'd better ask him,' Brooke said. 'He wants to help you.'

'He's not bloody coming again!' I knew I was shaking. 'He's not!'

Brooke watched me. 'Up to you. Now we'd better finish this physio session.'

I didn't want to. I didn't want to do anything except yell at everybody. But Brooke made me sit up, and we carried on throwing the plastic ball backwards and forwards. She wasn't as good as . . . as him.

RYAN:

Thursday, I had my first Defensive Driving lesson. I've no idea how I concentrated; I'd hardly slept Wednesday night. It was like those first nights, nearly three months back. Things were breaking apart again.

I didn't say anything to Mum when I got home from Watson House, but next morning she got so worried about how I looked that I told her. She said nothing at first, just hugged me. Jon nodded. 'Had to come out some time, mate.'

'The bad things are all over now, love,' Mum told me. 'Give Tara time. She'll feel different in a while.' But I knew she wouldn't want to see me again.

I got my first exam result back – eighty-six per cent for English. It didn't seem to matter much now.

'Good stuff, Ryan,' the teacher said. 'It's been an excellent term for you.' Yeah, well . . .

The Defensive Driving course was run by a guy who lived near the high school. There were two other people: an old woman who'd let her licence lapse, and a smart-arse guy about nineteen, who'd been up on a Drink-Drive charge. It was pretty interesting, really: all theory stuff on how to anticipate what pedestrians and kids and other cars might do, and what the worst distractions for drivers were. 'Chicks,' the smart-arse guy said, and smirked. I didn't say anything.

Then the instructor talked about what could make cars unsafe – how some guy liked going round an 80 km/h corner at 100 km/h, and one day he did it with two of his mates in the car. But their weight had changed the car's balance; it rolled and they were both killed. Smart-arse shut up after that.

When I got home, Mum was putting away her Office Skills stuff. 'Sally – Tara's mother rang,' she said. The same fear jerked inside me.

'They've been talking to Tara,' Mum went on. 'They wondered if you're free to go and arrange more physio with her tomorrow afternoon.'

TARA:

Mum came after breakfast. I ripped into her straight-away. 'I know who that Ryan guy really is. Why did you let him come? Why didn't you tell me?'

'He came because he asked and asked to, love. We didn't want to tell you at first because we couldn't know how much of a shock it would be.'

She started talking about some Family Conference, but I wasn't listening. 'He drives his bloody car into me, then he sucks up to everyone to make it all right!'

Mum shook her head. 'It's not like that. Ryan admitted it was his fault. He's never blamed anybody else.'

Somewhere in my mind, a blurry picture formed. Me, sprinting along a footpath and curving towards the crossing. I pushed it away. 'Why are you sticking up for him?'

'We're not, Tara. We're just sticking up for anything that makes you better.'

I glared at the wall beside her. Mum was silent for a second, then – 'At the start we were so angry with Ryan too, love. But he's going to live with this forever, just like you. So are his mum and stepfather.'

The 'stepfather' stopped me for a second. 'I don't want him here. The bloody liar!'

'That's up to you,' Mum said – just like Brooke. 'But he's not a liar, Tara. We asked him not to tell you.'

More silence. Mum took my hands, and I let her hold

148

them. 'Let's do some physio now, love. We can talk about it again later.'

Discovering that Ryan O'Carroll drove the car that injured her seemed to make the patient work even harder at her rehabilitation. This was unexpected but excellent. Her speech continued to improve. Her balance remained limited, especially when her left side had to take weight.

RYAN:

I drove across on Friday after school, feeling shit-scared again. Ash said at school (seventy-nine per cent for Geography – that's good) that Mel had told him about it, and he'd be there. Vince . . . huh, who's Vince?

When I walked into Tara's room, it felt like I was in court. She was in her wheelchair. Mel and Brittany sat there like Miss World and Miss Hitman. Ash leaned against the wall. There was no chair for me; I had to stand like someone in front of a firing squad.

'What are you doing here?' Tara went straightaway.

'Your mother said they wanted me to come.'

Brittany started in like I knew she would. 'She means why did you start creeping round here in the first place?'

I felt shamed, but I felt angry too. We'd already had this out, that time in *Burger King*. 'I've told you. Anyway, it's not you I –'

But Brittany interrupted me. 'Tell us again, eh? You've probably got a different lie from last time.'

Now I was really wild. She and I spoke together. 'I'm not –'; 'Bet you –' Then we both stopped as Tara went, 'Shut it, Britt. Let's hear him try to wriggle out of it.'

Brittany's face was pink. Mel watched, lips parted slightly. I looked at Tara. 'I'm sorry. I've told everyone that. I'd do anything if it could make things different. It was my fault.'

Brittany snorted. 'We know it's your fault. You sound like a bloody parrot!'

'It's not all his fault.' There was a second before I realised it was Ash speaking. The three girls' heads turned to look at him. I was still watching Tara, and a different expression seemed to flick across her face.

'Me and . . . we were mucking around,' Ash went on. 'Ryan was trying to stop us.'

Silence for a moment. At least I had one mate who'd stick up for me. 'That's no excuse,' Brittany grunted.

I started to lose it a bit. 'I'm not making a bloody excuse!'

'You better not be.' Her chin stuck forward. Her green eyes glittered. I felt a sudden weird respect for her. There was no bullshit with this chick.

Mel was still silent. Tara spoke again. 'You think you can make up for it by crawling round here lying.' Her voice wobbled; I could see she was gutted suddenly.

I tried to keep my own voice calm. 'No. I came because I wanted to do . . . anything. I told your –' I was going to say 'your parents', but I saw her face change again.

Brittany couldn't keep out of it. 'Well, she knows what you're like now, and –'

'Leave it, Britt,' Tara said again, and Brittany's face went pinker.

Tara's face was flushed, too. 'The –' She had to stop because her breath was coming so hard. The throat scar stood out. Slow down, I wanted to tell her. Breathe from the stomach, like in *TKD*. 'The only reason you're allowed here is to help me keep on with the physio.'

It took a second for her meaning to sink in. Then Brittany's mouth flopped open. Ash looked pleased. Mel looked the same – perfect. I hadn't a clue what I looked like, but I realised this part was over.

CHAPTER TWENTY-FOUR

TARA:

We didn't do any physio after that. I felt sick and dizzy, and things were blurry again. My arms and shoulders were sore; I'd been gripping the arms of my chair.

I got rid of them all. Britt seemed to understand, and said they'd push off and let me rest. He – Ryan – didn't argue. Ash went with Mel (funny, that).

They'd only been gone a second when Ash came back in. 'Didn't mean to get heavy, sorry. But Ryan's had a rough time too, eh?'

He's had a – I just nodded. 'You OK?' he asked. I mumbled something.

Shit, I thought afterwards. I'm supposed to be going to the last Summer League netball game a week today. Hope I can last through a bit of excitement by then!

RYAN:

We'd just got out into the hall when Ash said, 'Wait up', and went back into the nuclear blast zone. Mel suddenly said, 'Hope she's OK for the netball,' and smiled at me. 'You coming, Ryan?'

I had this sudden weird picture of Tara in her wheelchair, trying to play. Straight after it, another picture came. Brittany meanwhile was firing up. 'He's not –' She stopped as Ash came out, and we moved on down the hall.

Then I heard myself speaking. 'Do . . . ? You could try . . .' The others stared at me till I'd finished. Mel gave me another smile that showed her dimples. Ash said, 'Cool, mate.'

But Brittany was best. She just stood there with her mouth open. That made two – no, three times in the last half-hour someone had shut her up. Brilliant.

I drove home. Jon and Mum were going round to Pio's place for the evening, so it looked like another exciting Friday night at home by myself. Then about half-seven, the phone rang. Vince. 'Doin' anything?' he asked. 'Thought I'd drop by.' I was too surprised to know what to say. So I said yeah.

He came round quarter-of-an-hour later, with a couple of beers. We talked about nothing much for a bit, then he asked, 'How's Tara?'

I looked at him for a moment, then I told him. Vince sat there looking awkward. 'Sorry, mate,' he mumbled when I'd finished. 'I know I handled it bad. But the old man told me to keep out of it, eh? Said anything might happen, and I'd better stay low.'

'No worries,' I said, and half-meant it. Suddenly I felt so pleased I had Jon and Mum.

'Hey,' Vince said then. 'That Mel chick. I hear she's getting a bit bored with old Ash. Wants some excitement. Reckon I could excite her?'

I looked at him again. I let him rave on. When he

was leaving, I asked what he was doing the next day – Saturday. Vince looked a bit edgy. 'Might see ya,' he said. I went, 'Yeah. OK,' and left it like that.

I felt . . . sad, I guess. Like I say, there'd been a time when we planned to do everything together. Now – maybe I should have just told him to get lost. But we go back a long way. Yeah, I've said that, too.

Attention now turned to the patient's return to school after the holidays. Her accident had meant a serious setback. Handwriting problems meant she might need to use a keyboard in all classes. This and short-term memory problems could affect the subjects she was able to take. However, there was no doubt that her strength and fine motor tuning were steadily improving. She was now able to use a knife and fork to cut up most of her food.

RYAN:

Tae Kwan Do on Sunday. Good session. School on Monday. Eighty-one per cent for IT. Ohhhh-kay!

Yeah, I was trying to make myself feel good. Because Mrs Gower rang on Sunday and asked if I could do a session with Tara on Monday afternoon. Mum took the call and came back smiling. 'She sounds like there's a ten tonne weight starting to lift from her shoulders.' Yeah, and there was one just landed on mine.

In the foyer of Watson House, I ran into Brooke. She nodded at me. 'You just do all you can to help her. This isn't about making you feel better.'

Tara was on the side verandah of Watson House, with lawns and flower beds around. 'Hi,' I said. She said nothing, just wheeled her chair past me and headed towards the physio room. I felt my face go hot. Fine by me, I thought.

And it was, in some ways. I didn't have to talk to her about anything. 'We want to work on Tara's balance,' said Brooke. She showed me the exercises – Tara kneeling on the floor, lifting her arms one at a time, then her legs one at a time.

I managed OK. That *Tai Chi* stuff from Ze Minh helped – focusing and taking it slowly. She – Tara was good. She stuck at it. She's heaps better every time I see her. I had to hold her hips again; part of the time her leg was pressed against mine. She must have felt it; I certainly did.

After a bit, her left arm started to shake. 'You want to stop?' I asked. She snapped, 'I'll tell you when!' That was our big conversation for the day.

When she was in her wheelchair again, I asked, 'You want to go back to your room, or the verandah?' She shrugged. So I just walked out of the physio room without her. In the hall, I counted up to five, went back in to where she sat staring at me, wheeled her out onto the verandah, left her there. And I didn't feel bad about doing it.

TARA:

My body is so much better. I'm getting a bit of tone back into my muscles. I did a sort of fast walk along the verandah on Tuesday, holding the wall. A fast hobble, anyway. I had to stop at the end and pant. I'm not so good at other things: When I read a book, I keep forgetting what happened a couple of chapters back. That's another thing I've missed out on.

Britt and Mel came over. They lost on Saturday; The Rockets have fizzed to about halfway on the table. I'm definitely going to watch the final game this Friday. Brilliant!

'Is Ash coming?' I asked Mel, oh-so-casually. She shrugged. So it was like that, eh? Poor Ash.

I kept thinking how he came back into my room last Friday, after he'd stuck up for Ryan. And how Ryan behaved then and Monday. Walking out of the Physio Room and leaving me like that, after what he's done! Guys need a bloody good kicking, like Britt would say.

A rehabilitation programme for the patient, after she returns home, must be planned. Contact must be made with her school, so teachers understand the difficulties she will face.

RYAN:
I had my second Defensive Driving lesson on Wednesday. Smart-arse wasn't there. We looked at ways of checking the road for dangers before they happen. What do you do when the door of a parked car starts to open? When a kid is playing with a ball on the footpath? 'It's a different way of seeing,' said the Instructor. Yeah. That's happened to me in other ways, too.

School prize-giving next week. I'm getting a couple of certificates! Jon said we'd get takeaways to celebrate. I wanted *McD's*, but Jon said there was this great fish and chip place he'd heard about. Since he was paying, I couldn't argue. He phoned the order through, told me how to get there, and I set off in the *Subaru*.

It wasn't far from Lithgow Street, which is a name I'll never forget. I parked and went in, and there was Ze Minh looking at me across the counter.

'Hi, Lion,' he said. 'You come for Jon's order?' I stared, swallowed, and thought – You crafty sod of a stepfather.

Ze Minh chatted away about *Tai Chi*. 'I am really please you help Tara with her recovering,' he said. His wife smiled and said, 'Good. Good.' When he handed me the order and I asked how much, Ze Minh shook his head. 'No. You already paid.' I was driving home before I understood.

TARA:
He came over on Thursday afternoon, too, and we did the same exercises. I managed better than last time, but he still had to help me. He's got nice hands, all right. Nice lying-shit's hands.

He didn't say anything unless I did. Near the end, when we'd both been silent for about five minutes and Brooke was over the other side of the room, my mouth suddenly asked, 'Did I run out into the crossing?'

His hand went still on my arm. He said nothing for a second, then – 'It doesn't matter.'

'It does matter!' I began. 'If I –'

'No!' He spoke so loud, I got a shock. When I glanced at him his face was fierce, almost. 'I should have been paying more attention.' Another pause. 'I'm doing a Defensive Driving Course.'

'OK,' I went. I couldn't think of anything else to say.

When he was leaving, he looked at me. 'Enjoy the netball.' I felt surprised he'd remembered.

Mum and Dad picked me up after tea on Friday. I was so excited, I'd eaten hardly anything. Dad helped me into the car. Brooke had found a light wheelchair that folded into the boot.

It was my first night-time drive since the accident. The moment we stopped outside the Stadium (in the yellow wheelchair space – there are a few perks!) and I heard the thump of basketballs inside, I just ached to be out on the court.

All the Rockets were waiting inside the door. Ms Gilchrist kissed me on the cheek, asked, 'Where's your Maths assignment, Tara?' and kissed me again. The other kids hugged me. A lot of people smiled and nodded as Dad wheeled me to a place in the front row, right by the halfway line. Best seats in the house!

We watched the warm-ups. The Rockets were playing first, against another middle-of-the-table team. The result wasn't going to matter much, but I was so looking forward to the game.

The umpires came out and the teams took up their positions. There was a bit of a hush; both umpires had turned and were gazing towards the sideline. What –?

Then Dad stood up. He gave me a huge grin, and started wheeling my chair out on to the court. Clapping and cheering burst out all round the stadium. I sat with my mouth open while he pushed me into the middle.

Britt handed me the ball. She looked like she was going to howl. 'You throw off,' she said.

It felt awesome in my hands. For a second, I had this panic I wouldn't be able to do it properly, but his – Ryan's – exercises had helped, and I tossed a decent pass to Mel.

She stood smiling and holding it, while Dad wheeled me off the court, and the cheering and clapping went on. The game started. After a moment, Mum leaned across. She had been howling; I could tell. But she smiled now, and said, 'OK, love?'

'Yeah.' OK? I was bloody brilliant. 'Thanks,' I went. 'Cool idea.'

Mum and Dad looked at each other. 'Actually, it was Ryan's idea,' Mum said.

CHAPTER TWENTY-FIVE

TARA:

I took ages to get to sleep that night. The Rockets won; Ms Gilchrist said I must be their lucky mascot. I felt brilliant. But I felt crap, too. I watched them flying around the court and realised I've still got such a long way to go.

I felt crap about something else as well. The accident was mostly Ryan's fault. But I had something to do with it. I can't remember what, and I'm not going to ask. That'd just make things harder for Mum and Dad; I know that.

I thought about it over the weekend – when I had time to think. I had heaps of visitors. Mel and Britt came. Britt's doing Art Design next year, too. She says a lot of it's keyboard work, so I should be able to manage. Sweet. We talked about the holidays. I'm definitely going home for Christmas, then I'm back here – I suppose till they reckon I can handle things. And then . . . then I suppose I'll start finding out if I'll ever be 100 per cent OK again.

Mel went to the loo, so I asked Britt what the story was about Ash. Britt gave a bored sort of sigh. Mel gets up her nose sometimes. 'She's gone off him. That

Vince guy is sniffing around.'

I don't know any Vince . . . do I? I felt sorry for Ash. OK, he's quiet and doesn't seem all that exciting, but I like the way he thinks about other people. I suppose Ryan's like that, too, except when he's driving.

But I didn't have time to wear out my brain on that. Auntie Tamsin and Jarrod – Jonas – Jacob!! had driven all the way up, and on Sunday, they and Mum and Dad took me out for dinner at Jimmy's!

He'd closed the shop to other people, and stuck a notice in the window: SORRY: RESERVED FOR FAMILY FEATURE. Dolly had put a table out the front where customers usually wait. She smiled and smiled. The rest of us talked and talked. (Jimmy said he – Ryan – was in for fish and chips a few days back.) Dad took heaps of photos. He and Mum have made an album of me in hospital. I don't want to look at the early ones yet.

'When you were in I.C.U.,' Mum said suddenly, 'there was this young doctor. They called him an Intensivist, which always made me think of a sneeze. He was so good – he'd talk to us and to you. And one day, we were all just standing watching you, and the only sound was the ventilator helping you breathe, and this young doctor suddenly said, 'Man, I'm hungry! I could murder some fish and chips!' So I decided then that as soon as you could, we were coming here to Jimmy and Dolly's.' She turned and hugged them both. Hell, parents are embarrassing. But I guess I could have done worse.

Being at Jimmy's made me remember something else, too. Mum used to go on about how takeaways were bad for me. Now she and Dad are buying them for me!

RYAN:

I helped Jon shift stuff in the garage on Saturday. No schoolwork now exams are over. I'm going to get stuck in again next year; I want to try for journalism. I wondered suddenly what Tara wanted to do when she left school.

Sunday morning was *TKD*. The club's stopping soon for Christmas, and I coached the juniors for a demo they're doing on our last night. At the end, the little kid Sonja, gave me a martial arts magazine and said, 'Thank you for teaching me'. So I gave her a full *Tae Kwan Do* bow – feet together; arms by the side; bend over from the waist – and she giggled all the way out of the hall.

I hung out with Ash on Sunday afternoon. He's pretty down; Mel's told him she just wants to be friends. Jeez, I'd hate it if a chick told me that! I couldn't help thinking – so she's available, except I wouldn't have a hope against Vince. Anyway, I don't know if it's her . . . I'll think it out while we're at Pio's uncle's whatever's place.

It felt weird, me trying to help Ash get over something. After the way he's stuck by me, I was glad I could.

By this stage, the patient could walk by herself on even surfaces, though she still had difficulty walking while carrying anything. Her short-term memory continued to improve.

RYAN:

I went across on Monday afternoon. (Just a week and a bit of school left! I still hadn't heard if there was going to be a court case.) She was on the verandah in her wheelchair again, wearing shorts and a top. Her skin's a bit pale, which isn't surprising, I guess.

'Hi,' she said, which was an improvement on the last times. Then she asked 'How were the fish and chips?' I must have looked gobsmacked, 'cos she smirked and told me how she'd been to Ze Minh's.

'So how were yours?' I asked back. She looked serious and said, 'Jimmy's keeping the job for me. It'll be a while, though.'

I wheeled her to physio. Brooke said she wanted more ball-tossing, for arm and back strength. 'Watch where you're reaching,' I told Tara. She gave me a glare – I can see why she and Brittany are friends – and grunted, 'Yeah, yeah'.

Again, she was heaps better than last time. Her throws were almost real throws now. Half-way through the session, as she chucked one at me, she asked, 'Why did you get them to set up that throw-off? At basketball?'

I didn't realise she knew. I got a shock and dropped the ball, which made her smirk again. I thought you might be feeling left out. Like I –' Then I shut up.

She said nothing for a couple more throws, then she asked, 'This Vince guy. You know him?'

Oh no, I thought. Don't tell me you fancy him, too.

TARA:

I wish I was out of Watson House.

They've been brilliant, but I want to start living again, get back to my friends, work, netball, school . . . guys.

I keep thinking about Ryan, and that business about the netball game. Not many guys would have thought of that. Ash reckons he's a good mate. Brooke likes him. Dad and Mum reckon he's faced up to things.

Jeez, I don't fancy him, do I? Nah, it'd be too sick for words, fancying a guy who put you in hospital.

RYAN:
School prize-giving on Tuesday. I didn't get a couple of certificates after all. I got three!

Vince sat next to me in the assembly, and made a big deal out of pretending to go to sleep during the speeches. Mum came along; I saw this huge smile on her face when I was up on stage. She did the decent thing afterwards, and didn't make any fuss in front of my mates.

I went to the last Defensive Driving lesson after school on Wednesday. The old woman and I sat a test. What should you do if a car drives right up behind you? (Slow down so there's room for him ahead; wave him past when you can.) If a cyclist is hogging the middle of the road in front of you? (Treat him like a car; wait till there's no traffic coming before you pass.) If a car comes towards you in a narrow street and another car overtakes it, also coming at you? (Flash your lights, blast your horn, pull right over – even on to the footpath if it's safe.)

I did OK. The Instructor wished me good luck. I asked about the smart-arse young guy; he just shook his head and said, 'Some of them reckon they know it all.'

Thursday afternoon, I went to Watson House again. So did Ash. When I told him I was going, he said he'd meet me there. Suppose the poor guy hoped he might run into Mel. I was doing a bit of hoping, too.

'Who's a popular girl then?' Brooke smiled when Tara and Ash and I came into the Physio Room. Tara walked there by herself – slowly, but she did it.

Brooke wanted us to work on general co-ordination: things to get Tara using eye-limb sequences and moving several muscle groups at once. So I had this brilliant idea – get her to do some basic *TKD* patterns. Ash held her elbow in case she lost her balance, while I showed her how. She had problems standing on one foot, but she's got good focus, all right.

We'd been going for about ten minutes when Ash said, 'Tara's getting tired.' She was, too, though she wouldn't have admitted it. I'd been too wrapped up in the *TKD* to notice.

She sat down, holding on to the sides of the chair like she still does. 'That was cool. I'd like to learn *TKD* properly.'

I got this light feeling in my stomach; that's the only way I can describe it. 'I'm gonna be away for a week next Thursday,' I gabbled.

Brooke came in then, and I told her about being away, too. 'We'll have to find you another personal trainer,' she said to Tara.

Then Ash spoke. 'I'll help, if you like.'

We all looked at him. 'Excellent,' Brooke said. 'OK with you, Tara?' Tara shrugged. Yeah, sweet, I thought meanwhile. She'll be safe with Ash.

CHAPTER TWENTY-SIX

RYAN:

Friday afternoon, I phoned Ash to see if he wanted to hit Southside Plaza. 'I'll ring Vince too, eh?' I said, then wished I hadn't. Sure enough, Ash hesitated. 'Think I'll give it a miss.' I did some tossing-up in my head, and I tried Vince. 'Could have something lined up,' he told me. Shit, I'm a social failure.

But I went anyway, 'cos Mum wanted me to pick up some Christmas lights. I took the *Subaru*, and, as I came into the car park building, I saw a little kid standing by a car with his mother, while she loaded things in. I slowed down, like I'd learned in Defensive Driving, and suddenly he started trotting out into the traffic-way. I had plenty of time to stop – I probably would have even if I hadn't slowed. His mother grabbed him and gave me this embarrassed look. I drove on with my stomach churning.

Inside the Plaza, I was passing *McD's*, and there were Mel and Brittany at a table. I wasn't sure what to do. Mel saw me, and smiled. Then I was sure what to do.

She gave me another smile as I sat down. Brittany's face had no expression. I hoped Mel might say what a

166

cool idea Tara starting off the netball game had been, but she talked about the holidays, how her parents both worked, how it was boring with nothing to do. She looked around a lot, like she always does. She's got nothing to do, I started thinking. Hey, I could – Then Mel stared past me and went, 'Hi!' A voice I knew said, 'Hi' back, and Vince sat down beside us.

Yeah, he had something lined up, all right. I half-expected him to look shamed, but no way. Absolutely no way. He was off, talking and grinning to Mel. He took no notice of Brittany, and hardly any notice of me. Mel laughed and blushed and looked awesome. Brittany glared into her thickshake. I sat there like a spare sock, watching my ex-best mate perform. Yeah, I'd found out the truth about him, all right.

After maybe five minutes, Vince asked, 'Want to check out a few shops?' Mel went, 'Cool', told us 'See you guys soon', and they headed off, shoulders almost touching. I sat there like a spare used sock.

'What a sleaze,' muttered Brittany. I opened my mouth to tell her he was my –. Then I shut my mouth again.

Silence for a bit, except for Brittany working on the last of her thickshake. Then, still staring down into it, she said, 'Your netball idea was cool.'

I goggled at her. After a second, she went on. 'She's always been my best friend. When she . . . when I thought she was going to die, I was so scared what might happen to me.'

I nodded. 'The night it happened, I got home and started punching and kicking the door. I wanted to hurt myself, too.' Hell, I'd never told anyone else that.

'So you bloody should,' Brittany grunted. She looked up at me, said, 'I meant what I said at that Family Conference', and stared into her thickshake again. 'I was watching TV when Mel phoned about Tara getting hit. I didn't take on what she was saying at first – I was pissed off with her for interrupting my programme. I felt like crap about that, afterwards.' She glanced at her watch. 'I gotta go. I'm seeing this guy about a part-time job.'

Man, who would want a lethal weapon like Brittany working for them? Then as I drove home, I thought, Hey, she'd be perfect for Ash. He needs a chick with a bit of go. Mel was so hot, and friendly enough, but – yeah, I really knew it now. She didn't have guts and she wasn't staunch. Not like Tara.

The patient's parents were advised that steps, shower floors and uneven paths might cause difficulty for the patient at home. She would need assistance outside the house, and must not cross any roads by herself.

RYAN:

Ash came round on Saturday night. I didn't say anything about Mel or Vince. Mum and Jon were out again – hell, they've got a better social life than me. They'd left some salad and stuff. I took one look at it, and Ash and I headed off to Ze Minh's.

We stepped inside, and two customers turned from the counter. Tara's mother and father. 'Hello,' said Mr Gower. 'Someone else treating themselves?'

I didn't know what to say at first. I introduced Ash to them. 'Oh,' Mrs G said, 'Tara's new physio!' She and

Mr G looked heaps better. I remembered meeting them those first times in the hospital. I remembered bawling when Tara's mother hugged me. Jeez, how shaming.

'So you're off for a week?' Mr G was saying. 'Have a good time.'

'Thanks.' I remembered my manners and said, 'Hope Tara enjoys being home.'

Her mother beamed. 'It's our best Christmas present ever.'

TARA:
Britt came round on Saturday. 'Mel's out with that Vince,' she told me. I wasn't really surprised. Mel's cool, but when it comes to guys, well . . .

I told her how Ash was going to help with my physio. 'Suppose it gives him something to do,' Britt said. 'Jeez, thanks!' I went, and we both laughed.

Sunday, Mum and Dad took me for a drive to Puketapu Park. We sat on a bench and watched people, while they kept asking was I too hot? Too cold? Getting hungry? Getting queasy? Jeez, I thought: give it a rest, guys! But I didn't mind too much.

I keep going over the things I can remember. There's heaps I've forgotten, but I remember flying through the air; that drifting and floating feeling; voices; spewing up; moving to Watson House; knowing who people were – especially some people. I remember stumbling on the crossing. I guess that was my eyesight too. Hey, someone should write a book about me!

Ryan came on Monday, with Ash. He and Brooke showed Ash how to do some of the exercises. Ash isn't as good as him, but I suppose he'll improve. He doesn't say much. Ryan seemed sort of nervous again, like when he came those first times. At the end, he hung around for a second, then he said, 'See you in a week, then. I . . . let us know if you're still interested in trying *Tae Kwan Do*.'

Yeah, I told him. Yeah, I would.

To assist hand-eye co-ordination and short-term memory, the patient could start a journal in which she keeps details of her progress, treatment, etc. This should also help her to measure her own improvement.

RYAN:

Tuesday was the final *TKD* session for the year. The juniors did their demo, all of them in a line, going through their basic kicking, punching, blocking patterns. They looked good – must have had a brilliant instructor, eh?

A lot of their parents had come to watch. After they finished and bowed to Greg and broke up, the little kid Sonja's dad hugged her, and tossed her in the air so she squeaked.

Hell, don't drop her, I thought. I look at people now – especially kids – and I think how easily they can break.

We're off to Pio's uncle's place tomorrow.

TARA:

I've been making a list of what I want to be able to do. Read a book and remember it. Write properly – I've done some Christmas cards, and my handwriting looks like a pissed spider. Get my lenses, not get tired, play netball. Be my real self again. I am going to be 100 per cent. I've made my mind up.

I still get down sometimes. Or I get frustrated, which is probably better. I'm glad Ryan's away for a week. It'll give me time to make my mind up about . . . things.

Britt and Mel came. Britt's got a job for the holidays – helping Jimmy!! It's just till I can go back. Brilliant. Mel went on and on about Vince: his CD collection, his dad's big car, the party he's taking her to this weekend. Britt rolled her eyes at me again. Like I said, I felt sorry for Ash. Then suddenly I thought – hey, he'd be perfect for Britt! I'll have to try and get them together somehow. Why hadn't anyone else had this awesome idea?

Ash came on Wednesday. He was pretty shy, but Brooke showed him what to do for the exercises and stuff, and he picked it up fast. Physio is a great way to get groped by guys!

While Brooke was down the far end of the room, I asked Ash about Ryan. I'd planned it out. Seems they've known each other for ever. 'He's a top guy,' Ash said. I liked that.

'How about Vince?' I asked. I wasn't thinking – except I had to meet this Mr Cool sometime. Then I saw the expression on Ash's face. If my balance had been good enough, I'd have kicked myself. 'Sorry,' I gabbled. 'I didn't mean . . . I just wondered . . . how long you've known him – you and Ryan – I mean?' Oh brilliant, Tara. Bloody brilliant.

Ash didn't look at me. He was watching my balance as I leaned from one side to another. After a second, he said, 'About four – five years, I suppose. He and Ryan and I hang out everywhere together. Used to, anyway.'

You know that feeling when you know something has already happened to you? Somebody speaks, or you see something, and it's all been there before. It was partly like that when I looked up at Ryan's face after I fell from the chair, and realised who he was. Now Ash's words had made it happen again. This time, it was the front-seat passenger in the car I was seeing.

CHAPTER TWENTY-SEVEN

RYAN:

We left early on Thursday. Too early! Jon drove. When I'd woken up properly, I checked out any chicks we passed. Two or three months back, I thought I'd never be able to look at a girl again. I thought about Mel. Yeah, she and Vince would be perfect for each other. I thought about Britt and Ash.

After an hour, we turned off the main road and Jon asked if I'd like to drive. I eased the *Subaru* over a twisty road between scrubby hills. I'd been driving for maybe ten minutes, feeling good about it, when I saw this car coming up behind us.

It was a young guy – for a second, I thought he was Smart-Arse from the Defensive Driving course – with a chick beside him. He was really tearing along. The moment he caught up, he started swerving out to pass; then he had to pull in 'cos there was a corner coming up.

I checked him in the mirror as we went round a couple more bends. He was glued on my back bumper. 'You got an idiot behind you,' Jon told me, and I grunted.

We came to a straight bit. I indicated and started pulling over like the course had told me, but he didn't wait. He shot out and started tearing past me. For a second, I glimpsed the girl looking embarrassed, then a truck came round the corner ahead.

Because I was already slowing down, I stopped easily. The truck braked and veered over, jolting along the rough edge, twisting away from the ditch. The guy's car swerved and skidded, and slewed to a halt, facing across the road just a couple of metres from the truck. It stood there for a moment, then its wheels spun and it roared away, fishtailing round the corner ahead.

The truck came slowly on till it was opposite us. The middle-aged guy in it was red-faced and furious. 'Bloody young maniac!' He looked at me, nodded, and said, 'He's lucky you were driving sensibly.'

I drove on, more carefully than ever. Jon patted my shoulder. 'Great, mate.' Mum said, 'Oh, Ryan, you were so calm.'

'Thanks,' I muttered. I was picturing that chick's face, and another face. If I ever met that young guy again, I'd bloody murder him.

TARA:

I might write a book about me. Watson House have got me started on a sort of diary, and it's quite cool – even if my handwriting isn't. I've been writing about that Vince guy, and putting a few things together: that other face beside Ryan in the car; Ash saying they'd been mucking around; Britt reckoning he was a slimeball. He had something to do with the accident, all right. But I can't be bothered with him now.

I felt half-scared Mel and he might drop by. If they did, I'd ignore slimeball like he's never been ignored before. I tried to feel angry Mel was going out with him, but that's just her. I looked at Brittany when she came, all staunch and no bullshit. I remembered her face when I started that netball game, and I remembered another time, when she'd howled and howled after her puppy was run over. Hope she and Ash can get together.

When he came on Thursday morning, I didn't mess around. We'd only been in the physio room for about five minutes when I asked, 'Vince made the accident happen, didn't he?'

Ash said nothing. He was supporting me while I was on my hands and knees, doing the lift-one-arm-and-one-leg exercise. I got wild suddenly, knocked his hand away, and nearly fell over. 'Wake up, why don't you! He's a creep!'

Brooke pretended not to hear. Ash looked at me. He's got brown eyes, like mine, but his are sort of calm. 'If it was you and Britt (ha, he does like her!) and Mel, would you drop them in the crap?'

I didn't know what to say. I looked down at the floor; I was still kneeling. One of his hands was close to me. He's got nice hands, like Ryan, but longer and browner.

'Look,' he said, after another pause. 'Vince has got the looks, the mouth, the rich old man. Ryan's clever; he does *TKD*. I'm just their mate. They're the big thing in my life. OK?'

I thought of me and Mel and Britt. Guys are thick as shit, but they can surprise you, sometimes. 'Yeah,' I said. 'OK.'

RYAN:

It was a cool week at Pio's uncle's place. It was a big shed with a kitchen and verandah added on. There were three or four others like it scattered around, and a couple of new places perched up on the hill, looking a bit silly.

We were just fifty metres from the beach. I slept on the verandah, and the first morning I woke up, there was this enormous sky and horizon, all filling with pink and green light. The last stars went out, the world turned gold-and-blue, and the sea sighed on the sand down below. I lay there, thinking of the times three months back when I was awake and Tara was unconscious while the sun rose. I never want to live through days like that again. Yet in a funny sort of way I don't want to forget them, either.

Mum and Jon did boring middle-aged stuff: they walked, and talked, and read, and played cards. Me? I walked, and talked, and read, and played cards. Plus I ran and I trained for my *TKD* grading. I made some money, too. A guy two sheds along was building a new fence. We got talking, and since I'm an expert in putting fences up (and letting them fall down, though I didn't mention that), I ended up working a couple of mornings for him. He paid me sixty dollars! I can start building up my savings account again.

I thought about Tara heaps. Yeah, I'm going to see if she wants to go out with me. Maybe it's sick. Maybe she'll spit in my face and say it's disgusting. Whatever.

I felt calm after I'd made my mind up. I felt calm the whole week we were there, like you do when you've been really sick and you're recovering. But if I ever see that young guy in the car again, I'm gonna whack him.

After a closed head injury, the patient should not drink any alcohol for two years at least, and preferably never again. The importance of staying fit was also emphasised – not a problem with this patient. She intends to start swimming when she goes home. She also asked about netball. Any decision on contact sports should wait a few months.

The patient can now stand with eyes closed for some time before feeling giddy. After her life-threatening injuries thirteen weeks ago, this has been an excellent recovery.

TARA:

Mum and Dad are so excited about my coming home over Christmas. So am I; I can't wait to see my room again.

Ash came on Monday. And on Tuesday. And on Wednesday. He's been here almost as much as Mum and Dad and Britt. I've asked him about Ryan, like I planned, but most of the time we just yak about schools and movies and friends and bands. (He likes Thrash Metal stuff. I nearly told him I was a bit of a Head-Banger myself, but that would have been too stupid.) Once you get him going, he's really easy to talk to.

Wednesday morning was when it happened. Brooke had asked Ash to help with balance and leg-strengthening exercises. So I did some squats. The very first time I tried these, a couple of weeks back with Brooke, my left arm flopped around like the Kung-Fu Hamster's. And my left side was so weak then, that I kept toppling sideways. Today I was a bit tense, like I always am when I have to think about my balance, but it went fine. 'Good,' Ash kept going. 'Good.' He's really patient.

'I'm going to start swimming when I get home,' I told him. 'Get some tone back in my muscles.'

'You look fine to me,' Ash said. 'For someone in your condition, I mean.'

I stared at him. Was he trying to take the piss or something? Then I saw how embarrassed he was. 'I mean when you think what you're like,' he mumbled. 'What you'd normally be, I mean.' He stopped and thumped himself on the head. 'Oh, bugger!'

I started laughing. I laughed till my face went red and I thought I might topple over like before. Ash stared. Then he grinned. (He's got a nice grin, and a nice mouth.) Then he laughed.

'I've – I've gotta sit down,' I finally managed to gasp. Ash looked worried. He reached forward and took my elbows to help me up. His face was right in front of mine. Suddenly we both stopped laughing. We stared at each other instead.

Oh shit, I realised. Oh shit, oh shit.

RYAN:

We got back Wednesday afternoon. Tara should be going home in the next couple of days, so I'd try to see her tomorrow. I rang Ash to see how the physio had gone. He didn't say much – even for him – but yeah, Tara was OK.

'I'll see you tomorrow then,' I told him. Ash was silent for a second, then went, 'Yeah. Cool.'

Jon reckoned we had to finish the week with

takeaways, so he sent me and the *Subaru* and some money off to Ze Minh's – Jimmy, Tara calls him. I walked in, and there behind the counter was Brittany.

I stood with my jaw scraping the vinyl. Hell, I thought, it had to be her I was looking dopey in front of! She grinned, I suppose because I was looking such a retard. 'Sorry,' she said. 'Children need a note from their parents.'

She told me how she was just working there till Tara got properly better. We actually talked while she wrapped orders for a couple of other customers.

'How is Tara, anyway?' I asked. 'I'm going to see her tomorrow. Ash said she's been doing OK.'

Brittany glanced down. She must have guessed about me and Tara. Or – hey, maybe things had worked out, and she'd clicked with Ash! 'Yeah, she's cool,' she said. 'She's going home for Christmas the day after tomorrow.'

'Seen anything of Mel and Vince?' I asked. This was so weird; we were almost behaving like civilized people. Brittany shrugged. 'They're an item – today, anyway.' We both laughed – incredible!

Ze Minh came through with my order. 'Herro, Lion,' he said. 'Melly Christmas.' He shook hands with me, which felt cool. Brittany gave me another, awkward sort of grin. That made two smiles from her: Christmas must be coming, all right.

Next morning, I thought about ringing Vince and didn't. I rang Ash, but his sister said he'd already left. Jon needed the car, so I had to catch two buses to Watson House. I sat working out exactly what I was going to say to Tara. I was nervous, but not the sick nervous I'd been those other times when I was heading to see her. If Ash was there, I'd have to think up some way to get him out of the room.

In the front hall, I met Brooke. 'Hi,' she greeted me. 'Good holiday? Tara's on the verandah.' As I started off, she said, 'Your friend's there, too. Ash. He's been great.'

Yeah, I'd have to make up some excuse to get Ash out of the way, all right. I went slowly down the hall, practising how I was going to ask Tara to a movie or *McD's* when she was able to. I stepped out on to the sunlit verandah. Tara was there. And Ash. Sitting together and holding hands.

CHAPTER TWENTY-EIGHT

TARA:

His face changed. He looked at our hands, at me, at Ash. Ash started to pull his hand away, but I held on to it. I wasn't doing a Mel (shit, that sounds bitchy) in front of Ryan, but he had to know.

I'd understood it all suddenly. Not just that I fancied Ash, but if it had been Ryan instead, and if it became a long-term thing, then what happened to me would always be there between us. It wouldn't be fair – to Mum and Dad, to his mother and stepfather, to anybody.

I don't really hold anything against him anymore. He could even be a friend, some time. But that's gotta be all.

RYAN:

I'd had so many jolts in the last three months, I didn't think anything could get to me any more. But when I saw the two of them like that, my whole body seemed to go dull and heavy.

She knew. I could tell that. Ash looked shamed at first, then he was just quiet and calm. He was Ash. But Tara talked more than she'd ever done before, like she was trying to make it a bit easier for me. Her voice goes flat sometimes; when she gets up, she still staggers. But she's a real chick; funny I noticed it now more than ever.

She asked about the holiday, told me how she's going home tomorrow afternoon for Christmas, said Mel was wild at Vince 'cos he'd been chatting up some girl at the party they went to. Ash spoke a couple of times. I mumbled something; I dunno what.

Then Brittany arrived. I felt better that someone else was there. I saw the look she gave us, and understood why she'd seemed awkward at Ze Minh's last night.

'I like your top,' Tara told her, the way chicks do. Britt had a green T-shirt thing, the same colour as her eyes, I suppose. She glanced at me for some reason. 'The fish and chip smell gets into all my stuff,' she told Tara. 'I keep having to change. I can't stay long, eh? I'm helping Jimmy and Dolly at lunchtime.'

We agreed Jimmy and Dolly were cool. 'I'm teaching Dolly to say 'Girls Rock',' Brittany said. 'She goes 'Girls Lock'!' It wasn't much of a joke, but we laughed anyway.

Another couple of minutes, and I'd had enough. 'I'll see ya.'

Tara nodded, then she asked, 'You going to come and help Ash with the physio after Christmas? He's a slow learner.'

She stopped, and looked embarrassed at what she'd said. Brittany stepped in quickly, as if nobody wanted a silence. 'Two guys? Jeez, you're a bit greedy, Tara!'

I didn't even bother to laugh this time.

'Merry Christmas, eh?' Tara said as I was going. I managed to say it back. 'Merry Christmas.'

I wandered down the front drive. I knew I had no right, but I felt stupid. Totally bloody stupid. Mel and Vince; Tara and Ash, me and zilch. And I'd really thought . . . I stopped and did a half-hearted side-kick at a shrub. Then another. And another, hard. Twigs and leaves flew in the air.

'Vandal!' came a voice. Brittany. Shit, it had to be her again. How long had she been watching?

'You helped Tara heaps,' she said, as we stood at the bus stop. I started to grunt something, but she cut me off. 'No, shut up and listen! She says it's been really good. She wants to stay friends.'

Friends! I knew I'd hate it if a chick said . . . I opened my mouth to tell Brittany, then I remembered what she'd said about her and Tara. I shrugged instead.

Her bus arrived to take her to Jimmy's. 'See ya, eh?' she said. 'Merry Christmas.'

I managed to say it a second time. I hung around at the stop for another couple of minutes, then I thought, screw the bus anyway, and started a long, useless walk home.

TARA:
Mum and Dad didn't stop grinning for the two-and-a-half days I was home – except for when they had a row over whether we should have dinner outside or inside. It was cool to hear them arguing.

'I used to stare out of the window when you were in Ward 11,' Dad said when we were in deckchairs out the back on the first afternoon. 'There was this house

183

where the people used to sit on the back porch and talk. I told myself that you were going to do that by Christmas. Fathers are always right, eh?' Yeah, yeah, I thought. I stuck my tongue out at him.

It was an awesome Christmas, just me and them and Auntie Tamsin and Jacob. (Of course I know his name!) I felt wrecked, though. I've got a long way to go before I'm properly fit again. I fell asleep after lunch both days.

But I'm getting better all the time. A bit here; a bigger bit there. I'm going to set myself targets and write them in my journal. I'm definitely going to make that 100 per cent.

Ash rang on Christmas night, and we talked. Mum and Dad were dying to know what's going on, but I didn't tell. A girl's gotta have some secrets.

Mel and Britt came round on Boxing Day morning. Vince didn't. From the way Mel talks, I mightn't ever meet slimeball Vince; she was moaning how he's always going on about himself. Britt and I swapped secret grins.

Oh, and my secret didn't stay a secret for long. Ash arrived that afternoon – and the first thing he did was make me do some exercises. Mum and Dad grinned and left us to it. I felt a bit annoyed that he was here just for the physio, then I realised that the stretching and stuff gave him the chance to hold my hands, so . . . so I stopped feeling annoyed.

I got tired, and he saw it. 'Say hi to Ryan,' I told him when he was going, and he didn't seem to mind. Then I crashed for two hours.

Oh, and there was this really gross moment when I

woke up. I wandered out the back, with my mouth feeling like kitty-litter. Mum was in the garden, snipping tops off old roses and dropping them in a bucket. 'What are you doing?' I asked. (Yeah, real intelligent.)

Mum went, 'Oh, hello, love. I'm just trimming these. It's good for most things to get dead-headed.' She froze suddenly, and shot me this totally horrified look. I burst out laughing, and pulled a zombie face at her. Mum came over and hugged me till I thought I was going to suffocate. Then she tipped the bucket of old roses over me.

I didn't sleep much that night. I lay in bed thinking how brilliant it was to be in my own room, hearing the trees stirring outside. The night was quiet and gentle; it felt like time was slowing down for a while.

Three-and-a-bit months ago, I nearly died. Nobody's said so – not in those words. But I know. I was on the edge of a cliff, and I could have gone either way. It's made things seem special. I look at faces and pictures and leaves – I'll look at them better when I get my contacts! – and they seem so amazing. Hope it'll last.

Big thoughts, eh? I'm going back to Watson House tomorrow. Probably be another couple of weeks before I'm strong enough to come home for good. Ash is coming to see me. And Britt, and Mel. Cool.

I yawned and turned over. My left leg and arm are much better now. I slept.

RYAN:

My Defensive Driving Certificate was waiting for me when I got home. And the Youth Aid Officer rang to say he was pleased with how things had gone. That made me feel a bit better. Still no word from the cops. If I do have to go to court, then I'll make Vince . . . maybe.

Christmas was good. Jon and Mum and I didn't give each other much – we're all a bit short after what's happened in the last few months. But Mr Non-Event sent me a few bucks, which was more than I expected. We got a card from Tara's parents, too: BEST WISHES. Mum was pleased.

Pio came round. 'My uncle says you left the place really tidy,' he told Jon. 'What is it with you guys?' Some of Jon's other ex-Road Rager mates dropped in, too. I kept wanting to grin when I heard them going 'please' and 'thanks' as Mum served them Christmas cake.

I went for a run. I trained twice a day. I'm not gonna droop. Tara fought back, and I'm going to. Shit, when you think what she's missed out on, I had nothing to feel down about! Yeah, if I told myself that often enough, I might start to believe it.

Ash arrived Christmas Day afternoon. We sat around for a bit, then he went, 'Sorry if I messed things up between you and Tara, eh? It just sort of happened. I didn't know if you fancied her or not.'

'No worries,' I told him. I might believe that too, if I said it often enough.

Anyway, I didn't mind acting a big hero for the sake of my mate. It made a total of one person I was a hero for.

Boxing Day, I went for a run past Jimmy's fish and chip place. A sign read CLOSING FOR HOLIDAYING

TILL REOPENING JAN . . . I wondered what Brittany was doing.

I was helping Jon adjust the points on the *Subaru* after lunch when Mum called, 'Ryan! Phone!' As I came inside, she said, 'A girl. Hell, I thought. Tara? No, it couldn't be. I picked up the phone, and a voice went, 'It's Brittany here.'

I blinked and went, 'Hi! I was just thinking about you.' Then I had to tell her about running past Jimmy's. She was silent for a half-second, then she said, 'Tara's going back to Watson House tomorrow. She might be a bit down. You want to come and see her?'

At first I couldn't decide. Then I knew. 'Yeah. Yeah, sure.'

'OK,' said the voice on the phone. 'About two o'clock, eh?'

I took the *Subaru* next day. 'If the points cut out and it won't go, give us a ring,' Jon told me. Thanks, Jon. I drove carefully, the way I always do now, thinking of that Thursday night in the rain the way I always do, too.

A figure was standing by the car park entrance. It couldn't be. It was. 'Hi,' said Brittany. 'Thought I'd wait so I could ask you.' She hesitated, then – 'Any chance of my joining that *Tae Kwan Do* club of yours?'

My first thought was: our club's going to be busy, all right. I stared at her: the fair hair, the green eyes watching me. Then, suddenly, everything seemed clear, like a computer screen when it lights up in front of you. Suddenly I felt so bloody glad nobody had managed to get her and Ash together. 'Yeah. Sure,' I said. Inside my head, another voice was going Yeah! Sure!

We walked up the drive, not saying anything. The nurse Brooke was coming down the front hall. 'Hello, you two. Tara's round the side.' She smiled at us. 'She's a special girl. We'll be sorry to lose her.'

There were noises coming from the side lawn. As Brittany and I came through the double doors, we saw Tara standing under a basketball hoop fixed to the front of a big tree. Ash was passing her the plastic physio ball. The noise was coming from Mel, clapping and laughing and putting on a big act for Vince. Yeah, Vince! He was out on the lawn too, looking as edgy as hell while nobody else took any notice of him.

Tara set herself and threw. It was a good throw; my physio work had helped, all right. She staggered a bit, but the plastic ball curved up, rolled on the edge of the hoop for a second, then dropped through.

'Go, Rockets!' called Mel. Ash grinned. Vince still looked like he didn't know what to do.

Something pinched my elbow. I looked down, and Brittany was gripping my arm, staring at Tara. She looked like she was tossing up whether to cheer or howl. 'Yes!' she breathed. 'Yes!' She realised I was watching her, let go my arm, and looked embarrassed. Then she glanced at me and smiled.

I gazed across the lawn at my two, changed friends. At Tara, lurching slightly as she turned to grin at her friends. I thought of all the time ahead, and all the time she had to win back. I said it to myself. 'Yes.'

When she was admitted to Intensive Care three months ago, the patient's chances of survival, let alone a normal life, seemed slim. But skilled help, the love of family and friends, plus her own determination have seen it happen. The road to full recovery may take years, but youth and courage are on her side.

Good luck, Tara.

Useful links

www.nrsi.org.uk
www.thinkroadsafety.gov.uk
www.rospa.org.uk
www.direct.gov.uk/Topics/Motoring
www.larsoa.org.uk
www.dft.gov.uk/stellent/groups
www.transportdirect.info
www.bikesafe.co.uk
www.dsa.gov.uk
www.protectchild.co.uk
www.highwaycode.gov.uk
www.iam.org.uk
www.irso.org.uk
www.nationalsafetycameras.co.uk
www.basiccharity.org.uk
www.pbs.org/wnet/brain
www.msnbc.com/modules/brain
www.braininjury2000.info
www.thephysiotherapysite.co.uk
www.nhscareers.nhs.uk/nhs-knowledge
_base/data/4903.html
www.headway.org.uk
www.brainhelp.co.uk
www.equip.nhs.uk/topics/neuro/injury.html
www.cbituk.org

aurora metro press

Founded in 1989 to publish and promote new writing, the press has specialised in new drama, fiction and work in translation, winning recognition and awards from the industry.

Novels for young people

Sobibor by Jean Molla **ISBN 0-9546912-4-5 £6.99**

Thistown by Malcolm McKay **ISBN-0-9546912-5-3 £7.99**

Sacred by Eliette Abecassis **ISBN 0-9536757-8-5 £7.99**

Plays for young people

Warrior Square by Nick Wood **ISBN 0-9546912-0-2 £7.99**

Harvest by Manjula Padmanabhan **ISBN 0-9536757-7-7 £6.99**

The Dutiful Daughter by Charles Way/Mandarin translation by Yang Lijun **ISBN 0-9546912-6-1 £7.99**

Under Their Influence by Wayne Buchanan
ISBN 0-9536757-5-0 £7.99

Trashed by Noël Greig **ISBN 0-9546912-2-9 £7.99**

Lysistrata – the sex strike by Aristophanes, adapted by Germaine Greer and Phil Willmott **ISBN 0-9536757-0-8 £7.99**

Anthologies

How Maxine Learned to love her legs and other tales of growing up. Ed. Sarah le Fanu **ISBN 0-9515877-4-9 £8.95**

Theatre Centre: plays for young people introduced by Rosamunde Hutt **ISBN 0-9542330-5-0 £12.99**

Young Blood: plays for young performers ed. Sally Goldsworthy **ISBN 0-69515877-6-5 £10.95**

The Classic Fairytales retold for the stage by Charles Way
ISBN 0-9542330-0-X £11.50

Six plays by Black and Asian women ed. Kadija George
ISBN 0-9515877-2-2 £11.99

www.aurorametro.com